Porcelain

Pl. I

Porcelain

Hugh Tait

HAMLYN LONDON · NEW YORK · SYDNEY · TORONTO

Published by
The Hamlyn Publishing Group Limited
London · New York · Sydney · Toronto
Hamlyn House, Feltham, Middlesex, England
© copyright Paul Hamlyn Limited 1962
Reprinted 1963, 1964, 1966
Revised edition 1972
ISBN 0 600 37003 8
Printed in England by Sir Joseph Causton
& Sons Limited

Plate 1 *frontispiece*
Chinese celadon porcelain bowl of the Ming
dynasty (1368–1643), known to have been
brought back from a voyage in the Orient
undertaken by Count Philip von Katzenelnbogen
between 1434 and 1444; the silver-gilt mounts
were added soon after the Count's return–
certainly, before 1453 as is proved by the
enamelled coat-of-arms. The earliest piece of
Chinese porcelain to reach Europe which still
survives complete with its medieval European
mounts of precious metal. Ht. 20.6 cm. (8$\frac{1}{2}$ in.).
Hessisches Landesmuseum, Kassel.

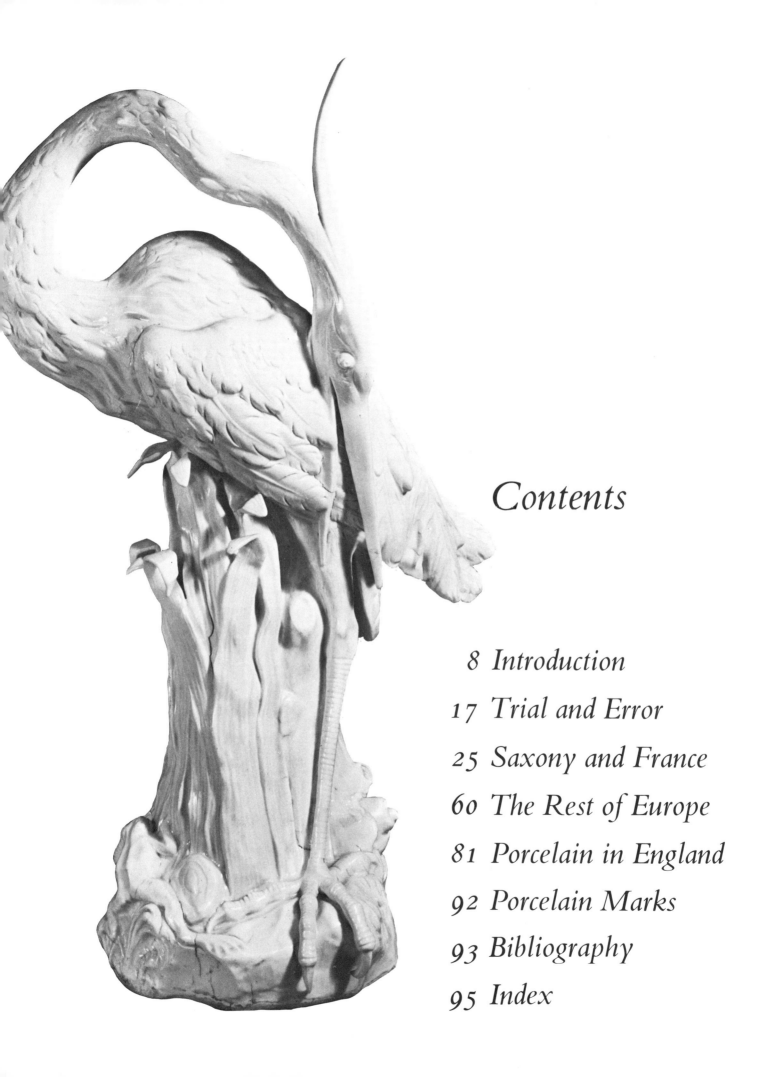

Contents

Pl. 2

Pl. 3

Pl. 4

Pl. 5

Plate 2

RIGHT Chinese porcelain bottle, decorated with Chrysanthemums in underglaze blue. Fourteenth century. Ht. 30.2 cm. ($11\frac{7}{8}$ in.).
LEFT Chinese porcelain bowl, decorated in underglaze blue, with a similar design at a later date. Mark: Chi'eng Hua (1465–87). Diam. 15.2 cm. (6 in.). Chinese porcelain of this type was reaching the Levant and being copied in Persia and Turkey. Both in the *British Museum, London.*

Plate 3

Medici porcelain ewer and dish, decorated in underglaze blue; made at Florence about 1575–87. Marks on reverse of dish: the dome of the cathedral of Florence and the letter F (in underglaze blue). The earliest porcelain to be made in Europe but only an artificial or soft-paste porcelain – not hard-paste or true porcelain like the Chinese. Ewer: Ht. 16 cm. ($6\frac{3}{8}$ in.). Dish: diam. 25 cm. ($9\frac{3}{4}$ in.). *British Museum, London.*

Plate 4

Pot, decorated in underglaze blue, probably made by Louis Poterat at Rouen about 1685. The earliest porcelain to be made in France but like the Medici products Rouen porcelain was an artificial or soft-paste porcelain. Ht. 13.7 cm. ($5\frac{3}{8}$ in.). *British Museum, London.*

Plate 5

Salt-cellar and a cup and saucer, decorated in underglaze blue; Marks on bases of all three pieces: the sun (in underglaze blue) made at St Cloud, near Paris, about 1700. Because the cup fits into a raised wall in the centre of the saucer and is, therefore, very steady, this type is known as 'trembleuse', for even a person with a shaky trembling hand can scarcely upset the cup. Salt-cellar: Diam. 8.5 cm. ($3\frac{3}{8}$ in.). Cup: Ht. 7.0 cm. (3 in.). *British Museum, London.*

Introduction

The Chinese had for centuries known how to make porcelain, that hard, thin, translucent pottery, by fusing china-clay (kaolin) with china-stone (petuntse) at a very high temperature. Supplies of these two essential ingredients, kaolin and petuntse, were found in one part of China, far inland in the Province of Fukien at a very early date (*c.* AD 900) and, having discovered the unique qualities of the wares produced by firing them together in extremely hot kilns, the Chinese proceeded to guard their secret most rigorously.

The first European to see Chinese potters at work was most probably Marco Polo. Whilst he was working in the service of Khublai Khan (1275–92), he visited the Fukien Province and he describes the strange Chinese ware being made by the potters in a place he called Tingui; the name he gave it was *pourcelaine*. This word, which in his day meant 'sea-shells' or 'mother-of-pearl', has taken on the new meaning bestowed on it for the first time by Marco Polo. When this great adventurer returned home to Venice in 1295, he assuredly brought back with him some pieces of Chinese porcelain. Tradition says that the small white bottle of Chinese porcelain with Ying ch'ing glaze in the Treasury of St Mark's, Venice (Fig. 1), is one of the pieces brought home by Marco Polo from his travels; it could well be true.

Throughout the Middle Ages, vessels of Chinese porcelain reached the princely courts of Europe, where they were so prized that they were mounted in gold or silver-gilt and richly ornamented with enamels and pearls. The ewer illustrated in Fig. 2 is the most famous example; known to us only from a water-colour drawing made by Gaignières in 1713, this ewer was afterwards lost, and when it was re-discovered in 1959 in the National Museum of Ireland, Dublin, the precious silver-gilt enamelled mounts were missing. The Dublin Museum had obtained it, already stripped, from the Hamilton Palace sale in 1882, though why and how the mounts came to be removed remain a mystery. The porcelain body (Fig. 3) now proves to be a hard white paste belonging to a small experimental group of porcelains made in or near Ching-tê-chên in Kiangsi Province during the first half of the fourteenth century by Chinese potters who radically altered the ceramic traditions of the Sung period (AD 960–1279). The heraldic coats of arms and the inscriptions indicate that the silver-gilt mounts were almost certainly added in Budapest by order of Louis the Great of Hungary (1342–82) as a gift to Charles III of Durazzo, when the latter successfully forced Pope Urban VI to crown him King of Naples in 1381. The goldsmith in Budapest, possibly a German craftsman, drilled a hole in the side of the Chinese bottle and converted it into a 'Gothic' ewer. As the only fourteenth-century example to survive – in part, at least – from the many pieces of Chinese porcelain which must have come through the Levant into Europe's great trading centres, Venice, Pisa and Genoa, this ewer is an historic document.

The inventories of the plate of the powerful French princes, like the Duke of Normandy (1363) or Jean, Duc de Berry (1416), prove that Chinese porcelain was among their most treasured possessions. The Chinese celadon porcelain bowl in the Landesmuseum at Kassel mounted in silver-gilt bears the arms of Count Philip von Katzenelnbogen as borne before 1453 and is the earliest example to survive intact (Plate 1).

Twenty pieces of porcelain were considered a suitably exotic gift for an Egyptian sultan to give to the Doge Pasquale Malipiero of Venice in 1461 and again later to the great Lorenzo de' Medici of Florence in 1487. In Italy, if not north of the Alps, lesser men than princes were beginning to savour the delight of eating from porcelain tableware: Nicolao Nicoli, a Florentine scholar, is said by Vespasiano da Bisticci in his *Lives of Illustrious Men* (written 1482–98) to be so cultivated that 'the whole of his table was covered with vessels of porcelain'.

By the second half of the *quattrocento*, the translucent Chinese Ming porcelain (Plate 2) was in plentiful supply in Egypt, Syria and Turkey, countries with whom the Italian merchants traded on a large scale; not unnaturally, many examples entered Italy and made their presence felt. Even the Italian potters, whose new and exciting tin-glazed earthenware with polychrome decoration, maiolica, echoed every Renaissance art motif, design and aspiration, paused at the height of the Renaissance

Map labels: 30, 20, 10, 0, 10, 20, 30, 40 (top); 60, 50, 40 (sides); GREAT BRITAIN, DENMARK, SWEDEN, RUSSIA, UNITED PROVINCES, AUSTRIAN NETHERLANDS, FRANCE, SWITZERLAND, AUSTRIA, BOHEMIA, ITALY, PORTUGAL, SPAIN. Cities: Liverpool, Stoke-on-Trent, Longton Hall, Derby, Worcester, Lowestoft, The Hague, Swansea, Cardiff, London, Bow, Chelsea, Tournai, Plymouth, Bristol, Rouen, St Cloud, Chantilly, Paris, Sèvres, Mennecy, Cologne, Hochst, Würzburg, Frankenthal, Ludwigsburg, Nymphenburg, Munich, Zurich, Turin, Vinovo, Milan, Padua, Venice, Florence, Doccia, Rome, Capodimonte, Naples, Madrid, Buen Retiro, Furstenberg, Berlin, Limbach, Meissen, Dresden, Fulda, Prague, Vienna, Copenhagen, Stockholm, Marieberg, St Petersburg (Leningrad). Scale: 0 100 200 Miles. GATRELL 30

(*c.* 1510), to include an ornament which they called *a porcellana*, a running band of foliage in the Chinese manner using the Oriental monochrome blue technique.

In the same exciting century, the *quattrocento*, the Venetians were discovering the secret of making beautiful, clear, thin, feather-light glass and of embellishing it with colours. Venice was quickly to become Europe's envied home of glass-making, but it was in Venice that the translucent glassy quality of Chinese porcelain was first keenly appreciated and envied.

Here in Venice began the two-hundred-year quest by Europe to discover the Oriental secret of porcelain. That patron of the arts, Ercole d'Este, Duke of Ferrara, purchased seven bowls of *porcellana contrefatta* (counterfeit porcelain) whilst visiting

Venice in 1504. Leonardo Peringer, a mirror maker, stated to the Senate in Venice in 1518 that he could make 'porcelain of every kind, like that called Levantine'. However, the very few surviving specimens suggest that the Venetian experiments used opaque white glass and not clay or potters' earth. Similarly, Camillo da Urbino and his brother Battista, who were engaged in 1561 by Duke Alfonso II of Ferrara to make maiolica and porcelain do not seem to have had any real success before all experiments were abandoned in 1571.

But within the next few years a partial success was to be achieved at the Florentine court of the Grand Duke of Tuscany. In 1570 Cosimo de' Medici, the grandson of Lorenzo il Magnifico, achieved his great ambition to be crowned Grand Duke, the first in the Florentine republic. Cosimo pursued the

9

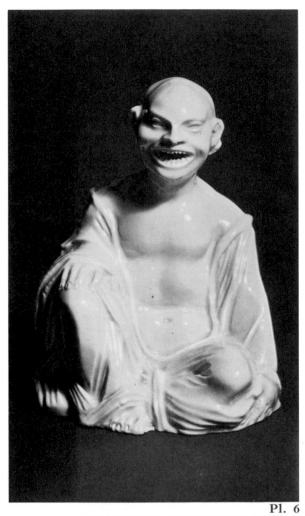

Pl. 6

Pl. 7

Pl. 8

Plate 6
Figure of a Chinaman squatting; hollow and thin; no painted decoration; made at Meissen about 1715. Engraved on the back: $N = \frac{220}{W}$ the inventory mark of the Japanese Palace Collection belonging to Augustus the Strong in Dresden. The earliest porcelain figures made in Europe. The Chinese originals are said to represent the Chinese god of Voluptuousness and the Meissen copies may have been popular as a lover's present. Ht. 9.5 cm. ($3\frac{3}{4}$ in.). *British Museum, London.*

Plate 7
Cup and saucer, enamelled with the coat-of-arms of Sophia, Electress of Hanover (died 1714) and (on the reverse side of the cup) a flowering tree; made at Meissen before 1714. The earliest painted example of porcelain made by Böttger at Meissen. Saucer: Diam. 13.5 cm. ($5\frac{1}{4}$ in.). Cup: Ht. 8.3 cm. ($3\frac{1}{4}$ in.). *British Museum, London.*

Plate 8
RIGHT Flower-holder, decorated in underglaze blue and gold (only traces of gilding now survive) and enamelled in puce with the monogram CBM and (on the reverse) a coat-of-arms. Inscribed in puce (on the base): *Vienne 12 Julij 1721.* The earliest dated Viennese porcelain with painted decoration. Made by Du Paquier at Vienna in 1721. Ht. 23.5 cm. ($9\frac{1}{4}$ in.).
LEFT Jar with cover, enamelled in puce with St James the Greater and (on the reverse) a saint kneeling before the Instruments of the Passion; traces of gilding on the masks and the cover. Made in Vienna about 1725. Ht. 15.5 cm. ($6\frac{1}{8}$ in.). *Both in the British Museum, London.*

Plate 9
Lantern from a gondola, decorated in underglaze blue and thin gilding; made at the Vezzi factory in Venice 1720–27. This appears to be the only surviving gondola lantern in porcelain–the porcelain lanterns made at Vienna are of a different shape. Ht. 31.1 cm. ($12\frac{1}{4}$ in). *Victoria and Albert Museum, London.*

Pl. 9

role of a patron of the arts and encouraged new artistic crafts in Florence, such as tapestry-weaving and *pietra dura* mosaic. From Vasari's second edition of the *Lives of the Most Eminent Painters and Sculptors* (1568), we learn that Bernardo Buontalenti 'in a short time will be seen making vessels of porcelain'. Buontalenti supervised all artistic ventures at the Grand Ducal Court and so, although great interest was focused on the Florentine experiments to make porcelain, none had yet been produced in 1568.

Cosimo's morose son, Francesco, who became the second Grand Duke from 1574 to 1587, was deeply interested in all these artistic pursuits. Without doubt, Francesco I de' Medici was personally associated with the success referred to by the Venetian ambassador to Florence, Andrea Gussoni, in a report written in 1575, which stated that Francesco had re-discovered the method of making Indian (i.e. Oriental) porcelain after ten years of research, and that a 'Levantine' had helped to make the experiments successful. But the Italian potter Flaminio Fontana, a member of the Urbino family so famous for its maiolica, must share some of the credit, for he was in Florence from 1573 and was paid for firing twenty-five to thirty pieces of porcelain.

With the death of Francesco I de' Medici in 1587, the manufacture of porcelain in Florence seems virtually to have come to a halt. Three men, the Grand Duke Francesco I de' Medici, Flaminio Fontana, the potter, and an anonymous 'Levantine' are the only persons who from the records can be closely associated with the first porcelain to be made in Europe, the so-called 'Medici porcelain' (Plate 3).

But, of course, 'Medici porcelain' is not true porcelain; it is not, like the Chinese, made from kaolin and petuntse. It is soft-paste porcelain, an imitation, artificial porcelain; in this case, it comprised a mixture of glassy materials (including white sand and rock-crystal) and white clay (probably kaolin) in approximately the proportions 12:3. Nevertheless, this 'Medici porcelain' was a great achievement, and we are fortunate that today there are fifty-nine recorded examples of this first European porcelain, of which only fourteen are at present unlocated. With the exception of a spouted jug in the Baron Maurice de Rothschild's Collection, which is painted in polychrome, with green, yellow and blue grotesques outlined in purple, all the other pieces are painted in underglaze blue only, that is to say, the transparent lead-glaze is applied after the vessels have been painted. None of the fifty-nine pieces is a copy of an Oriental form; many of the shapes are very simple, like the plates with the flattened rim and central boss (Plate 3), whilst others copy the fantastic details of Mannerist ornament which so often detract from the pure elegant grace of the High Renaissance forms.

Only in some of the painted decoration does the Oriental influence appear. The painted designs are

frequently typical Renaissance motifs, such as are to be found in the repertoire of any large contemporary maiolica workshop; but occasionally they are copied from the blue-and-white Ming porcelain (Plate 2) produced in the reigns of Chia Ching (1522–66) and Wan Li (1573–1619). More often, a design of foliage and flowers, winding asymmetrically over the surface with a soft undulating rhythm, can be found (Plate 3), and perhaps these designs are a delightfully new Florentine adaptation of the patterns on Persian wares or those on the Isnik wares from Turkey. Certainly, the painting is delicate and sensitive, and though derivative it has an individual quality, creating a style new in European ceramic art. The history of European porcelain would have been very different had the manufacture outlived its founder, Francesco I de' Medici. With so few pieces in the world today, it is hard to resist the almost magical quality that surrounds the very name 'Medici porcelain'.

Fig. 1
Chinese porcelain bottle with *ying ch'ing* glaze. Probably made in late thirteenth century. Traditionally described as one of the pieces of porcelain brought back from China by Marco Polo in 1295. Ht. 12.1 cm. (4¾ in.). *Treasury of the Cathedral of St Mark, Venice.*

Fig. 2
The 'Gaignières–Fonthill' Ewer–the earliest example of the European practice of mounting Chinese porcelain in precious metal. The silver-gilt enamelled mounts incorporate four heraldic charges and three inscriptions in gold Gothic characters, from which it has been deduced that the porcelain bottle was mounted in 1381 at the order of Louis the Great of Hungary (1342–82) to form a suitably splendid gift for presentation to Charles III of Durazzo, who had been crowned King of Naples in that year. This water-colour

drawing and the detailed notes made by Roger de Gaignières record the ewer as it looked in 1713, when in the collection of Louis XIV's son, the Dauphin. In 1822, the ewer had reached England and was one of the 'show-pieces' of William Beckford's collection at Fonthill. *Bibliothèque Nationale, Paris.*

Fig. 3
Bottle of Chinese porcelain which previously formed the body of the 'Gaignières–Fonthill' Ewer; a view showing the hole drilled for the silver-gilt spout. By 1882, when the National Museum of Ireland purchased it at the sale of the collection of the Duke of Hamilton (Beckford's son-in-law), the precious mounts were no longer attached. The porcelain bottle was made in or near Ching-tê-chên, Kiangsi Province, during the first-half of the fourteenth century. Ht. 28.3 cm. (11⅛ in.). *National Museum of Ireland, Dublin.*

What happened to the secret of making porcelain in Italy after the death of the Grand Duke Francesco I de' Medici in 1587 is a tantalising puzzle. A certain Nicolo Sisti is described as a potter of maiolica and porcelain in Florence in 1592 and at Pisa in 1619. At a great court festival in the Palazzo Pitti in 1631 all the noble guests were presented with tokens of 'Royal Porcelain' stamped with the Medici arms— none appears to have survived!

Two small soft-paste porcelain bowls, however, are preserved in the Victoria and Albert Museum; they are inscribed and dated, respectively, 'I.G.P.F. 1627' and 'C.G.P.F. 1638' (Fig. 4 a–c). Both are marked with a cross and a sign that appears to be copied from a Chinese character. They are both extremely light, of almost paper thinness and have a yellowish translucency. The later bowl is painted in underglaze blue only, but in addition to the blue there is, on the earlier bowl, an opaque yellow-brown in the centre of the tree-trunks, and a copper-green is used on the foliage and the birds. On the outside of the later bowl the sprays of hyacinth and other flowers are definitely copied from the Turkish pottery from Isnik.

Unfortunately, no other porcelain has been found which can be associated with these two irrefutably dated pieces. Because there is a resemblance between them and a class of Paduan maiolica of the first half of the seventeenth century, these bowls are thought to have been made in Padua, but at present they form little more than an intriguing sequel to the 'Medici porcelain'.

Plate 10

Two bowls; the Japanese original LOWER LEFT was made at Arita in the early eighteenth century, and the Meissen copy TOP CENTRE was made about 1725. Box, enamelled in the Japanese (Kakiemon) style; made at Meissen about 1725. Marks: both the Meissen pieces bear the 'crossed swords' mark: on the box in underglaze blue and on the bowl in over-glaze blue; in addition, the bowl has a very rare and elaborate large mark in gold and the initial 'H' (in underglaze blue). Original bowl: Diam. 13.0 cm. (5⅛ in.). Meissen copy: Diam. 13.5 cm. (5¼ in.). Box: L. 10.8 cm. (4¼ in.). All three, formerly in the Japanese Palace in Dresden. *British Museum, London.*

Plate 11

LEFT Coffee-pot, enamelled with designs based on the engravings of Johann Schmischek (1630);

Marks: crossed swords and the initial 'S' (in underglaze blue); made at Meissen about 1725. Ht. 16.0 cm. (6¼ in.).

RIGHT Tankard, enamelled with a 'chinoiserie'; the shield is inscribed: *George Ernst Kiel, Meissen den 6 Juli 1724.* Made at Meissen and painted by Johann Gregor Höroldt. No factory mark but painted in brown in cursive script: *George Kiel.* Ht. 16.5 cm. (6½ in.).

CENTRE Porringer and cover with pierced openwork handles containing the monogram FA (Frederick Augustus) which was only used by the Elector of Saxony for eight months between February and October in 1733. Made at Meissen for the Elector and enamelled with 'chinoiseries' by Höroldt. Marks: crossed swords (on the base in underglaze) and the numeral '2' (in gold) on the base and inside of cover. Diam. (with handles) 16.0 cm. (6¼ in.). *All in the British Museum, London.*

Fig. 4
Two bowls of Italian soft-paste porcelain with underglaze blue decoration; both marked (on base) with a cross potent and a symbol, perhaps a poor imitation of a Chinese character. Inscribed on base, respectively: 'I.G.P.F. 1627' and 'G.G.P.F. 1638'. Probably made by two potters, 'I.G.' and 'G.G.' of the same family, perhaps at Padua ('P.F.' standing for *Padorano fece*). Diam. 12.7 cm. (5 in.). (1627 example). Diam. 11.7 cm. (4⅝ in.). (1638 example). *Victoria and Albert Museum, London.*

Trial and Error in England and France
1665–1710

With the establishment of the Dutch East India Company at Hirado (Japan) in 1609, increasingly large and regular supplies of Chinese Ming porcelain arrived by sea, pouring into Europe through Antwerp and Amsterdam. The Dutch potters were content to produce tin-glazed earthenware (faience) versions of these blue-and-white pieces. In England and Germany, the potters followed suit, especially in London, at Southwark and Lambeth, and in Frankfurt-am-Main. The long drawn out disturbances after the collapse of the Ming dynasty in 1644 doubtless disrupted the export of Chinese porcelain.

In Europe, the middle decades of the seventeenth century were unhappy years for many countries, the Thirty Years' War (1618–48) bringing ruin to much of Germany, the Cromwellian civil war in England and the civil war of the *Fronde* in France, and in Italy the military campaigns of the French and the Spaniards. Whether or not these political and economic disasters are the underlying reason why no further experimentation or research into the secret of making porcelain was carried out, the fact remains that only in the atmosphere of relative stability and

peace that was re-established by about 1665 to 1670 in England under Charles II and in France under Louis XIV did interest in the mysteries of porcelain-making reappear. Of course, with the stabilisation of the Chinese kingdom under the Manchu emperor, K'ang Hsi, at the same time, there was a complete resumption of trade and a new wave of Oriental influence swept into Europe. By the last quarter of the seventeenth century, no palace, no large house, was complete without its Chinese room and a cabinet of Chinese porcelain. This new vogue stimulated fresh speculation about the process of producing this bewitching material.

In England, John Dwight (d. 1703), who had studied at Oxford and was known to the newly formed Royal Society, was granted on 23rd April 1671 a patent for the manufacture of 'transparent earthenware commonly known by the name of Porcelain or China and Persian Ware'. There is little doubt that Dwight very nearly succeeded in the manufacture of hard-paste porcelain at his pottery in Fulham, but his ignorance of china-stone (petuntse) was an insuperable obstacle, and so,

Fig. 5
Mug of thin white stoneware, partially translucent; two bands of horizontal reeding; silver-gilt mount. Attributed to John Dwight at Fulham, London, about 1680. The form of this tankard is found in fukien blanc-de-chine porcelain of the late 17th century. Ht. 9.1 cm. (3⅝ in.). *British Museum, London.*

Plate 12
Vase, with yellow ground colour. Mark: AR (in monogram) in underglaze blue; made at Meissen about 1730. Ht. 36.8 cm. ($14\frac{1}{2}$ in.). *British Museum, London.*

Plate 13
Vase, with underglaze blue AR mark; made at Meissen about 1735 and perhaps painted by Adam Friedrich von Löwenfinck. Ht. 34.9 cm. ($13\frac{3}{4}$ in.). *British Museum, London.*

Fig. 6
Mustard-pot of soft-paste porcelain with
silver-mounts; decorated in underglaze blue with
the arms of Asselin de Villequier of Rouen.
Attributed to Louis Poterat, the founder of the
Rouen porcelain manufactory, about 1680.
Ht. 9 cm. (3½ in.). *Musée National de Céramique,
Sèvres.*

Fig. 7

Vase of red stoneware, made by Böttger in about
1715. Fired at 1200°C; this non-translucent
pottery is of stone hardness and can be polished
on a lapidary's wheel. Ht. 63.0 cm. (25.0 in.).
Collection of Dr A. Torré, Zürich.

although he could control the very high temperature
required, he could not achieve more than a remarkably fine white stoneware of extraordinary translucency and thin crisp potting (Fig. 5).

Only two years after Dwight received his patent,
a French potter called Louis Poterat, who worked
in Rouen, was granted a patent for the manufacture
of porcelain. When he applied for the patent to be
renewed in 1694 it was stated that 'the secret was
very little used, the petitioners devoting themselves
rather to faience-making'. Louis Poterat claimed
that only he personally knew the secret and alleged
that the small quantity already produced was made
without any assistance from workmen. When he
died in 1696, 'crippled in his limbs by the ingredients
used in his porcelain', his secret was apparently lost,
for no other potter in Rouen ever attempted it. The
identification of this Rouen porcelain is extremely
difficult; evidently very little was made and even less
has survived. The silver-mounted porcelain mustard-pot in the Sèvres Museum (Fig. 6), with the
arms of Asselin de Villequier of Rouen, is thought
to be the most reliable example, for, apart from the
heraldry, it is painted in underglaze blue with a
design that is common on contemporary Rouen
faience, derived from the style invented by Bérain
and the designers of the court of Louis XIV. A
number of other similar pieces have been identified,
all painted in underglaze blue only (Plate 4). Again,
like the 'Medici porcelain' these Rouen pieces are
an artificial porcelain, the first examples of French
soft-paste (*pâte tendre*), which for nearly a century
was to be the only type of porcelain made in France.

In 1692, four years before Louis Poterat died, a
chemist called François de Morin submitted to the
Académie des Sciences a *Mémoire sur la fabrication de
la porcelaine*, and there is some inconclusive evidence
to link this Morin with the new porcelain manufactory at St Cloud, just outside Paris, which claimed
to have made since 1693 porcelain 'as perfect as the
Chinese'. This, indeed, was the verdict of an
English traveller, Dr Martin Lister, who visited the
factory in 1698 – but he also noted that it was sold 'at
excessive rates'. The St Cloud factory belonged to
the Chicaneau family, who had some connections
with Rouen. Certainly there is a resemblance
between the Rouen porcelain and the earliest products of St Cloud, between 1693 and 1720, which
are often decorated in underglaze blue with lacework borders of Bérain style (Plate 5). Both these
soft-paste artificial porcelains are similar to look at,
especially as the early St Cloud examples have a
more bluish-white tone than the later wares, which
have a warm ivory quality.

The factory had the protection of Monsieur, the
king's brother, and in 1700 the Duchess of Burgundy
was received at the factory by 'MM. Chicaneau'.
With the death of Chicaneau's widow in 1722, the
factory passed out of the family and a new chapter
in its production began.

Plate 14
Meissen porcelain, with different ground colours, made about 1725–35:
TOP Pot and cover, with enamelled and gilt decoration and applied white stalk handles; made of solid lavender-grey porcelain paste. Mark: crossed swords (in blue over the glaze). Ht. 11.5 cm. (4½ in.).
TOP RIGHT Four-lobed cup also made of a solid coloured porcelain paste with applied sprigs of white porcelain. Mark: crossed swords (in underglaze blue) L. 7.5 cm. (3 in.).

TOP LEFT Teapot with Kakiemon style decoration on a turquoise powdered ground. Mark: crossed swords (in lilac overglaze) and, in addition, the Japanese Palace inventory number. Ht. 9.5 cm. (3¾ in.).
MIDDLE LEFT Cream-jug, with monogram AR (Augustus Rex) in relief in white on a solid pinkish porcelain paste. Mark: crossed swords (in underglaze blue). Ht. 5.5 cm. (2¼ in.).
MIDDLE RIGHT Cup, with imitation Chinese mark (in underglaze blue), painted by Höroldt with 'chinoiseries' against a brown ground colour.

Diam. 7.9 cm. (3⅛ in.).
BOTTOM RIGHT Jug and cover, with harbour
scenes painted by C. F. Herold against a greenish
buff ground colour. Mark: crossed swords (in
underglaze blue); in addition an 'N' (in red over
the glaze) on base and inside cover. Ht. 11.1 cm.
(4⅜ in.).
BOTTOM LEFT AND CENTRE Cup and saucer, with
European figure scenes painted in the style of
C. F. Herold against a mauve lilac ground. Mark:
crossed swords (in underglaze blue). *All in the
British Museum, London.*

Plate 15
Coffee-pot, tea-pot and sugar-box, made at
Meissen about 1725 and enamelled later outside
the factory by a *Hausmaler*, probably in
Augsburg, about 1725. Most likely, they were
decorated in the workshop of Johann Aufenwerth
(died 1728) of Augusburg. Coffee-pot: Ht.
19.1 cm. (7½ in.). *British Museum, London.*

Saxony and France

Success at Dresden, 1710–20

The porcelain factory at St Cloud had another very important visitor: in 1701 Ehrenfried Walther, the Graf von Tschirnhaus, came west from the court of Saxony to examine at first-hand the successful French soft-paste manufactory. He was critical of it, declaring none of its products to be as good as 'real porcelain'.

Von Tschirnhaus, descended from an old Bohemian family, had left Leiden University in 1674 after six years of study, and travelled through Europe, coming in contact with the Académie des Sciences in Paris, with Leibniz in Hanover, and with Canon Manfred Settala of Milan, who had written about his own method for making porcelain. How strikingly similar are the background and milieu of the two contemporaries, von Tschirnhaus and John Dwight; neither was a potter and both were seeking the same knowledge, but neither was apparently aware of the other's existence.

As early as 1694 von Tschirnhaus had succeeded in convincing his prince, Augustus the Strong, King of Poland and Elector of Saxony, that his experiments might lead to the eagerly awaited answer. After his return from St Cloud, his efforts seemed to be more rewarding, but in 1703 Saxony's war with Sweden was going so badly that the Elector temporarily lost interest in the luxury of porcelain, with the result that von Tschirnhaus approached the Stadthalter, Prince of Fürstenberg, and Dresden came near to losing one of its chief claims to fame, that of being the home of the finest European porcelain. However, in 1704 Augustus of Saxony's interest revived and he gave von Tschirnhaus an assistant, Johann Friedrich Böttger, a chemist with a much tarnished reputation, whom the Elector had imprisoned.

In the new laboratory built by the Elector, these two men completed the experiments. At first, in 1707, they succeeded in producing a very hard, red stoneware, which so delighted the Elector that he provided a factory in the Venusbastei in Dresden (Fig. 7). The management of the factory was assigned to Böttger so that von Tschirnhaus could concentrate on his laboratory work. On 15th January, 1708, the first true porcelain was produced experimentally and in July 1708 von Tschirnhaus was made Geheimrat (Privy Counsellor) and director, but by October 1708 he was dead, without any acclamation as the discoverer of the secret of making true porcelain. Within six months of his superior's death, Böttger was able to announce to Augustus that he could produce a fine white porcelain, a suitable glaze and add the usual painting, so that it was to be 'as perfect as the East-Indian'. Böttger was technically the discoverer, and posterity has acclaimed him accordingly, but the laurels should more deservedly be bestowed on von Tschirnhaus.

On 23rd January 1710, the Royal Saxon Porcelain Manufactory was founded and established in the Albrechtsberg fortress at Meissen, near Dresden. Later in 1710, the new invention was proudly exhibited at the Leipzig Fair. It was, in fact, true hard-paste porcelain, like the Chinese. Tschirnhaus had found what was denied to Dwight, a supply of china-stone. In 1710, the white clay from Kolditz was replaced by finer clay from Aue, and in 1713 porcelain was at last produced on a commercial scale, the products being offered for sale at the Leipzig Fair for the first time that year. As early as 2nd May, 1711, Böttger sent a crate of his undecorated ware, valued at 462 florins, to Tobias Bauer, an Augsburg goldsmith, to be mounted in gold or silver and to be painted with gold or coloured scenes. Many examples of Böttger porcelain, with gold *chinoiseries* added in Augsburg, have survived (Fig. 8).

The cup and saucer in the British Museum (Plate 7) with arms of Sophia, Electress of Hanover, who died in 1714, is the only reliably dated example of the very earliest Meissen porcelain. It has not yet the pure white colour of the Meissen porcelain of the 1720s – there is a yellowish tinge. The enamel colours are sticky and stand out on the surface of the glaze. However, the porcelain is thinly and delicately

Fig. 8

Tankard of early Meissen porcelain, with two bands of horizontal reeding. Decorated with *chinoiseries* in gold in Augsburg, the silver-gilt mounts and cover are hall-marked: Augsburg and 'PS' (Paul Solanier, b. 1635, master 1665, d. 1725). Ht. 20.4 cm. ($7\frac{7}{8}$ in.). *British Museum, London.*

Pl. 1

Pl. 1

Plate 16
Pair of Chinese figures, made at St Cloud about 1735. Ht. 15.5 cm. (6⅛ in.). *Musée des Arts Décoratifs, Paris.*

Plate 17
LEFT Box, decorated with 'chinoiseries' executed in appliqué gold in relief and partially covered with translucent green enamel. Silver-gilt mount bears the Paris hall-mark of 1733–4. Made at St Cloud about 1730. The rare technique of appliqué enamelled gold relief decoration was first practised on porcelain by C. C. Hunger in Dresden about 1715. L. 8.9 cm. (3½ in.).
CENTRE Lid of a box, decorated with 'chinoiseries' on both sides in opposite directions; made at St Cloud about 1735–40. Diam. 7.5 cm. (2⅞ in.).
RIGHT Figure of a cat, couchant, and enamelled with 'chinoiseries'; made at St Cloud about 1740. L. 4.5 cm. (1¾ in.). *All in the British Museum, London.*

Plate 18
Figure of the God of Long Life, made at Chantilly about 1740. Ht. 20.0 cm. (7⅞ in.). *Musée des Arts Décoratifs, Paris.*

Plate 19
Dish, enamelled in the Japanese style; made at Chantilly about 1735–40. Mark: a hunting horn in red. At Chantilly a tin-glaze was placed over the porcelain, thereby providing a unique white ground for the enameller to paint on. L. 21.3 cm. (8⅜ in.). *British Museum, London.*

Pl. 18

Pl. 19

potted, and already a serious rival to the imported Oriental porcelain.

Böttger died in 1719, and in those six years when, under his direction, the Meissen factory was operating on a commercial footing, the quality of the porcelain steadily improved. The forms, however, were either Baroque silver shapes or copies of the Chinese, and the decoration tended to be limited to the Baroque lacework designs and restrained sprays of flowers–often in applied relief (Fig. 9).

Böttger did not attempt many figures in his new porcelain, though some were made from moulds taken directly from the Chinese originals, the *blanc de Chine* figures from Tê Hua Fukien. This figure (Plate 6), now in the British Museum, was in the famous Japanese Palace in Dresden–a vainglorious conceit conceived by Augustus the Strong, when he found himself to be the only monarch in Europe to possess a successful porcelain manufactory. For this purpose, Augustus acquired in 1717 the recently built Holländische Palais and renamed it the Japanische Palais, intending to put his vast collection of Oriental porcelain in it, reserving the upper floors for the products of his own Meissen factory. In the end, the Japanese Palace housed almost 40,000 pieces, which later formed the Porzellansammlung of the Johanneum (the Dresden Museum). From time to time duplicates from this collection have been sold, and consequently there are a number of pieces in the West, like this figure of the Chinaman in the British Museum, which bear the Johanneum inventory mark scratched into the glaze. The Japanese Palace Collection has remained to this day, despite the ravages of world wars, a magnificent tribute to the men who made 'Dresden China' so famous that even the Chinese were forced to copy it!

Piracy in Vienna and Venice, 1720–30

Despite the elaborate precautions taken by Augustus of Saxony to guard his secret of porcelain-making, which was confided under oath by Böttger, to only two other persons, some of the processes became known to a drinking friend of Böttger, Christoph Konrad Hunger, and in October 1717 Hunger was induced to desert from Dresden to Vienna by Graf von Virmont, the Austrian representative at the court in Dresden.

In Vienna, Claude du Paquier, a gentleman who held a very minor office at the Imperial Court, had been experimenting without success for several years. For some, as yet unknown, reason, the combined efforts of du Paquier and Hunger during the year 1718 were abortive, and in 1719, the year of Böttger's death, the Meissen kilnmaster, Samuel Stölzel, was lured to Vienna. With his help hard-paste porcelain was made in Vienna for the first time in 1719, and the second true porcelain factory in Europe was established.

But in April of the following year, Stölzel returned to Meissen, taking with him a gifted young enameller, Johann Gregor Höroldt, whose advent was to save the Meissen factory from the chaos that followed the double disaster of Böttger's death and Stölzel's defection, and to lead it swiftly to a pre-eminent position. Stölzel's farewell gesture to du Paquier was to spoil all the raw materials at the Vienna factory, doing damage estimated at approximately 15,000 florins. Within a few months, Hunger was engaged by the Venetian ambassador in Vienna and left the city for Venice.

However, bad as things were for du Paquier in 1720, he continued to make good porcelain, as is proved by the earliest dated decorated piece of Vienna porcelain, the flower-holder in the British Museum, which is inscribed: 'Vienne 12 Julij 1721' (Plate 8). Although a certain primitive quality in the potting of this piece underlines the severe loss experienced by du Paquier when his three technical assistants deserted him, the successful use of underglaze blue (a difficult achievement) and the accomplished overglaze painting in puce testify to a splendid recovery from great adversity. The porcelain itself is not unlike Böttger's, but in nothing else is the flower-holder reminiscent of Meissen.

With fresh financial backing–though no direct royal patronage–the factory developed a highly individual style, both in form and decoration, owing remarkably little to Meissen and rarely slavishly copying from Chinese and Japanese porcelain. Much of the decoration is derived from the engravers of Augsburg and southern Germany, and the several gifted painters, like Jakob Helchis, who were employed there after 1725, gave Vienna porcelain a unique style (Plate 8). Only after weathering several more crises did the enterprising du Paquier find security in 1744, when the Empress Maria Theresa took over the factory and had it run as a state enterprise under his management.

When Hunger left Vienna in 1720, he travelled direct to Venice, the city where the first European porcelain experiment had been attempted with glass over two hundred years before. He joined there a very rich goldsmith, Francesco Vezzi, who commenced the third successful true hard-paste porcelain factory in Europe. But it was to last for only seven years, for by the beginning of 1728 a financial crisis caused its closure. In those seven years, however, a true hard-paste porcelain of high quality was produced–often as good as the contemporary products of Meissen and Vienna. A remarkable–possibly unique–survival is the gondolier's lantern (Plate 9), on which the underglaze blue is quite as good as Meissen could produce. The use of a thin gilding with the blue gives a 'lustre' quality that is quite individual, and the employment of some very good artists, like Lodovico Ortolani, makes the products of this short-lived factory very desirable. Its sudden end was due in part to the treachery of Hunger, for he was back in Meissen in August 1727,

buying his pardon by informing the Meissen Commissioners that the Vezzi factory depended on imported china-clay from Aue in Saxony. In 1728, the export of this clay was forbidden by Augustus of Saxony.

Fig. 9
Teapot with applied flower-spray in high relief; no coloured decoration; made by Böttger at Meissen about 1715–19. Ht. 10.8 cm. (4¼ in.). *British Museum, London.*

The Painters' Period at Meissen, 1720–*c.* 1735

Significantly, Augustus the Strong's new name for his porcelain palace was the Japanese Palace – not the Chinese Palace! Though it is rarely appreciated, there was, in fact, far more Japanese enamelled porcelain entering Europe by the beginning of the eighteenth century than there was Chinese. Japanese porcelain from Arita and Kutani, often delicately painted in iron-red, turquoise, green, yellow and a lilac blue, with the slight asymmetrical designs named after the potter, Kakiemon, became most popular in Europe towards the end of the seventeenth century, when, for example, the royal collection at Hampton Court was formed during the reign of William and Mary.

The Kakiemon style is distinctive and in remarkably good taste, often leaving much of the white porcelain undecorated. This Japanese porcelain was rightly accorded equal status with the Chinese, and

the Meissen factory in the 1720s, like the contemporary French soft-paste porcelain factories, copied and then created endless improvisations on the Kakiemon themes (Plate 10), though not to the total exclusion of the beautiful Chinese blue-and-white or *famille verte* patterns.

When J. G. Höroldt joined the Meissen factory in 1719, his outstanding talents were, no doubt, used to buy Stölzel's pardon, for the latter was reinstated without punishment. Höroldt's skill and knowledge quickly endowed Meissen with an even more brilliant range of colours, and in 1723 Höroldt, at the age of twenty-seven, was appointed *Hofmaler* (court painter) and in 1731 he was put in charge of the forty painters of the factory. With Höroldt's strong, vivid palette and the improved whiteness of the paste, due to substituting a feldspathic rock for alabaster, the factory swiftly developed large export markets in France, Holland and Turkey.

Höroldt's enamel blue, achieved only in 1728, was never a complete success, and this colour is conspicuously absent on Meissen porcelain of this period. The underglaze blue, so perfect in the Ming porcelains, was equally difficult to attain, and Augustus offered 1,000 thalers reward for the dis-

covery. A reasonable quality was achieved as early as 1720, but frequently the blue turned a blackish blue of uneven, patchy quality, and in 1727 so deteriorated that it was abandoned until 1732. This setback also affected some of the Meissen versions of Japanese designs, such as the coiled phoenix pattern (Plate 10).

The two bowls of this design, now in the British Museum, both come from the Japanese Palace in Dresden; one is the Meissen copy. On the base of the Meissen copy there is painted the famous crossed swords mark, the Meissen factory's mark, which was first introduced in about 1724. The decision of 1723 to add a factory mark to the Meissen products was made partly out of a just pride in the quality now consistently maintained, partly that they should not be confused with the Oriental wares, but even more urgently that they should be distinguished from the growing number of pieces, even services, which were acquired by devious means from the factory in the white by independent enamellers for decorating outside the factory.

This outside painted decoration, or *Hausmalerei* as it is often called, has strong individuality, and such eccentricities and amusing characteristics that in its

best forms it is more highly prized today than the best factory painting. There is a vivid human element in this field, for a number of leading *Hausmaler* in Augsburg, Bohemia and Silesia have signed their best achievements, and so the style of Ignaz Bottengruber of Breslau, of Jucht and Metzsch of Bayreuth, of Ignaz Preissler of Bohemia and Johann Aufenwerth of Augsburg (and there are others) can be recognised and many pieces attributed to their workshops (Plate 15). From a collector's point of view the *Hausmalerei* has this distinct advantage over the relatively anonymous factory painting, although the technical quality of the *Hausmaler* rarely compares with the factory painting.

Höroldt also introduced into the Meissen repertoire a new type of polychrome decoration—little pseudo-Chinese figures, often silhouetted against the sky but at times set in an exotic Oriental landscape. These are *chinoiseries*—as opposed to the genuine copies of Oriental patterns, which were executed in a spirit of emulation or rivalry. These imaginary Chinese scenes are derived from the late seventeenth-century European spate of *chinoiseries* in the decorative arts, but Höroldt adds a touch of distinctive originality, so that this vast category of

Plate 20
Pair of toilet-pots in the form of boars, in a contemporary leather case, tooled to simulate books; attributed to Mennecy about 1740–50. Mark D.C.O. (incised). Ht. 22.9 cm. (9 in.). *British Museum, London.*

Plate 21
RIGHT Coffee-pot, decorated with blue stencilled floral design; made at Doccia about 1740. Ht. 23.8 cm. (9$\frac{3}{8}$ in.).
LEFT Bowl, double-walled, the inner painted blue, the outer in the form of an open-work coral trail; made at Doccia about 1745. Diam. 14.0 cm. (5$\frac{1}{2}$ in.).
CENTRE Bowl, double-walled, the inner painted blue to resemble marbling; the outer pierced in the form of a lozenged network, with four cameo medallions of Hercules and the Cretan Bull, Europa on the Bull, Venus and a Sea God. Made at Doccia about 1745. Diam. 8.9 cm. (3$\frac{1}{2}$ in.). *All in the British Museum, London.*

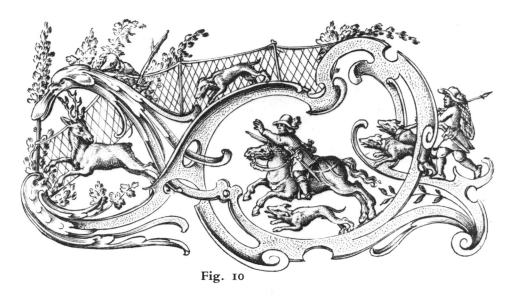

Fig. 10

Meissen porcelain (*c.* 1723–35) has a unique character.

One of the earliest–and certainly by Höroldt himself–is the tankard in the British Museum (Plate 11), enamelled on 6th July 1724 as a gift for Georg Ernst Keil, a relative of a leading Meissen citizen called Johann Gottlieb Keil, whose only daughter Höroldt married in 1725. The painting of the Japanese blossom sprays, in conjunction with these entirely European *chinoiserie* figures, is typical of the earliest J. G. Höroldt painting.

Another example of the Meissen painters' dependence on seventeenth-century engravings during the early period of Höroldt's advent is to be found on some Meissen porcelain gaily painted with a fantastic pattern of scroll-work with leaping figures

almost ensnared in them (Plate 11). The style curiously anticipates the Rococo in its exciting asymmetry, but the painting is most cleverly adapted from the engravings of Johann Schmischek, published almost a hundred years before (Fig. 10).

Höroldt's great achievement from his very first years at Meissen was to master the problem of ground colours on porcelain so brilliantly that no other European factory, not even Sèvres in the second half of the eighteenth century, ever produced so many–or any more technically perfect. The earliest to be mastered was the brown glaze, often referred to as the 'Chinese dead-leaf' colour; a cup with early J. G. Höroldt *chinoiseries* set against a sky of light billowy clouds is a perfect example (Plate 14, middle right). An early attempt to achieve

Fig. 11

Fig. 10
Engraving by Johann Schmischek (1585–1650); one of a series of ornamental designs published in *Neues Groteschgen-Büchlein*, about 1630. These engravings were adapted by the painters at the Meissen factory in the early period, 1720–30, (see plate 11), but very few–perhaps less than ten– examples are recorded. *Kunstbibliothek, Berlin.*

Fig. 11
Green bowl and cover in the style of contemporary Chinese porcelain. Formerly in the Japanese Palace, Dresden. Made at Meissen about 1730. Ht. 15 cm. (5$\frac{7}{8}$ in.). *Museum für Kunst und Gewerbe, Hamburg. Loan from Ernesto and Emily Blohm.*

Fig. 12
Heron, modelled by Johann Joachim Kaendler in December, 1731, and intended for the Japanese Palace in Dresden. Made at Meissen between 1731–5. Kaendler often sketched and modelled from the life at the *ménagerie* at Moritzburg and succeeded in imparting to his ceramic animals an uncommonly animated quality. Ht. 73.7 cm. (29 in.). *Pflueger Collection, New York.*

Fig. 12

33

Plate 22

Elephant, with housings and three 'chinoiserie' figures on its back; painted all over in green to resemble Chinese celadon; attributed to Meissen about 1730–40. In recent years, the attribution to Meissen has been questioned and a nineteenth-century origin has been suggested. However, one example (in the Forsyth Wickes Collection, Museum of Fine Arts, Boston, U.S.A.) is fitted to a gilt-bronze stand of elaborate Rococo design, which so exactly accommodates the four feet of the elephant that it would seem to have been made specifically for this figure; the gilt-bronze stand has been authoritatively identified as 'French and dates from around 1750'. (See *Burlington Magazine,* April, 1969, p. 217, fig. 45, and July 1969, p. 452; see also account by Carl Dauterman in *Antiques*, September, 1968, p. 347.) Ht. 30.5 cm. (12 in.). *British Museum, London.*

Plate 23

Chinese celadon porcelain vase; mounted in ormolu, perhaps by Jean-Claude Duplessis, of Paris, about 1740 to form an ewer. Ht. 30.5 cm. (12 in.). *Wallace Collection, London.*

a light turquoise green can be seen on a very small teapot (Plate 14, top left), painted with slight Kakiemon scenes in the reserved panels; the evidence of the technical difficulties facing Höroldt in these experimental days is also to be found on this piece, for after the kiln-firing the ground colour on the lid turned out more successful than on the body of the teapot, where it has darkened and crazed.

The yellow ground was much prized for its supposed Chinese 'Imperial' colour, and a splendid vase, brilliantly enamelled with large-scale birds and butterflies on the deep yellow ground without any reserves, is in the British Museum (Plate 12). It has the famous 'AR' monogram mark in underglaze blue, which was used for pieces intended for Augustus Rex himself or as royal gifts.

The Chinese were famous for their green celadon wares which were so much prized by the eighteenth-century European collector that they were frequently mounted in gilt-bronze (or ormolu). The effect, in the hands of great craftsmen like Jean-Claude Duplessis (d. 1774) in Paris, is exciting and beautiful (Plate 23), for the dull, gilt-metallic tone of the ormolu scrolls stresses the warm, soft shiny green of the plain and simple forms. No eighteenth-century European porcelain factory, except Meissen, is thought to have succeeded in reproducing the celadon glaze. The most bold example is as fine a piece of pure *chinoiserie* as can be found – an elephant with Chinese riders (Plate 22). However, the celadon effect is not achieved in the true Chinese technique of colouring the glaze but by painting on the white porcelain and covering with a transparent glaze. Certainly, Meissen, in attempting to produce a porcelain with green ground in the style of contemporary Chinese porcelain – not the celadon ware – created several very different tones of green; unfortunately very few examples have survived (fig. 11).

A few very rare pieces survive with a coloured porcelain paste – not merely a surface decoration – to prove that at Meissen Höroldt tried every means to achieve unique effects in coloured grounds. There are several pieces with a soft pink body, usually having the crowned monogram 'AR' applied on the side in white porcelain (Plate 14, middle left), which were made about 1725–30. Of the same date is the barrel-shaped pot and cover of a solid lavender blue-grey colour (Plate 14, top); the leafy stalk handles are applied white porcelain, like the handle and spout on the pink cream-jug. A miniature cup of a darker blue-grey coloured paste in the British Museum (Plate 14, top right) has applied sprigs of leaves and flowers in white paste porcelain. But the shape of the handle, the slovenly form of the crossed swords mark and the ogee quatrefoil form of the cup indicates a later date, perhaps about 1740.

Early in the 1730s the popular *chinoiserie* paintings of Höroldt underwent a change, developing into a miniature style within a frame, silhouetting the figures not against a painted sky, but against the white of the pure porcelain. The diminished scale for the figures can be observed on the porringer and cover in the British Museum (Plate 11), which can be exactly dated by the monogram 'FA' executed in porcelain in a unique manner within the openwork handles. When Augustus the Strong of Saxony died in February 1733, he was succeeded by his son, Frederick Augustus II, but on 5th October of the same year the new Elector of Saxony succeeded to the throne of Poland and was henceforth known as Augustus III, using the monogram 'AR' (Augustus Rex) like his father. The monogram 'FA' was in use for only eight months, during which time this bowl was certainly made and decorated by Höroldt for the personal use of his new master.

With the old Elector's death, however, Höroldt's significance began to fade, for it had been the Elector's insatiable passion for porcelain with magnificent colourful decoration in the Oriental style that had inspired Höroldt. The change in taste called for a new man, whose achievements were to steal the limelight, though Höroldt was still to produce very fine enamelled porcelain.

One of Johann Gregor Höroldt's best assistant painters was Christian Friedrich Herold, who was probably a relative and came from Berlin to Meissen about 1725. About 1730–35 he and his assistant copyists introduced into enamelled Meissen tableware a curious half-Europeanised *chinoiserie* set in harbour landscapes, which led on to one of the best-loved styles of Meissen painting – the so-called harbour scene style, with tiny European figures by wharf or sea-shore or in a landscape. One of the finest examples, probably by C. F. Herold himself, appears on a milk-jug with cover, with a most exceptional ground colour, a velvety greenish-buff (Plate 14, bottom right); remarkably large sprays of *indianische Blumen* are painted between the reserved panels directly against the ground colour with extraordinary effect. Another example, the work of Herold's assistant, can be seen on the cup and saucer with the mauve lilac ground (Plate 14).

Probably the most famous of J. G. Höroldt's young painters was Adam Friedrich von Löwenfinck, who began as an apprentice in 1727 and

Fig. 13
Tureen from the 'Swan Service' modelled by Kaendler in 1738 for Count Brühl and his wife and decorated with their conjoined coat-of-arms, Brühl-Kolowrat. Meissen; 1738. Mark: crossed swords (in underglaze blue). The 'Swan Service' is perhaps the most beautiful and magnificent table service ever to have been made by a porcelain factory – originally 2,200 individual items, Kaendler and Eberlein worked on it from 1737–41. The sauceboats in the form of swans, owing to the lavishly modelled decoration, carry no heraldic decoration. Diam. 48.3 cm. (19 in.).

deserted from Meissen in 1736 after a quarrel. Some have seen in the most splendid 'AR' vase in the British Museum (Plate 13) the work of Löwenfinck, though there is only stylistic judgement to support the attribution. Certainly the vase is an outstanding example of the quality that was being produced under J. G. Höroldt's direction in the 1730s at Meissen. Nowhere, not even at Sèvres, was there to be found large-scale porcelain decoration with such brilliancy of palette and originality of design.

Rivalry in France with Soft-paste Porcelain, – c. 1720–50

A renewed patent was granted in 1722 to the two new proprietors of the St Cloud factory, Henri and Gabriel Trou. With the added protection of the Duke of Orleans, the factory now embarked on its most successful period, for, although it did not close until 1766, its last fifteen years were sadly marred by a decline in quality. The great charm of typical St Cloud porcelain of the period, 1720–40, is its

Plate 24
Paroquet, made at Vincennes about 1745, in imitation of the Meissen birds modelled by Kaendler. Ht. 14.0 cm. (5½ in.). *Musée des Arts Décoratifs, Paris.*

Plate 25
Bolognese dog, first modelled by Kaendler at Meissen in 1741; this model remained so popular that the Meissen factory continued to produce this figure during the nineteenth century. Ht. 19.4 cm. (7⅝ in.). *Cecil Higgins Museum, Bedford.*

warm ivory tone, its satin-smooth texture and the sturdy vigorousness of its forms.

As at Meissen in these years, the enamelled decoration is frequently based on the Chinese and Japanese, especially the Kakiemon, but with a very different effect. Because the porcelain is soft-paste, the soft, fusible glaze–like an oily wax–allowed the colours to fuse deeply into it and, because of its low firing temperature, a wider range of colours of richer quality than at Meissen was possible. Although much was produced in the white in imitation of the *blanc-de-chine* figures and tablewares, the enamelled wares are the more enchanting (Plate 17). The factory evidently had a good modeller, some of whose improvisations are engaging (Plate 16), though the later Meissen copies are disappointingly lifeless.

Another French porcelain factory was founded near Paris at Chantilly in 1725 by the Prince de Condé, whose family château was there. Under the direction of Ciquaire Cirou, there was produced a unique type of porcelain, for over the porcelain he placed a tin-glaze, that is to say a glaze made opaque and milky white by adding tin-ashes, as the delftware, faience and maiolica potters did. This tin-glazed Chantilly porcelain is unparalleled; it is also among the most beautiful (Plate 19). Not only is the palette distinctive, but also the forms are often among the most delicate and graceful to be found in porcelain. The Prince de Condé had a very large collection of Japanese porcelain, which he and his contemporaries believed to be Korean. These items were made available for the Chantilly decorators to copy–hence the term 'décor Coréen' is still used to describe the Chantilly versions–but the master-painter at Chantilly possessed a truly brilliant gift for handling the Oriental designs and adapting them to the new shapes. The modelling of figures, as at St Cloud, was in this period restricted largely to the Oriental (Plate 18), and they are extremely rare.

The only other French attempt to produce porcelain in this period was carried out under the protection of the Duc de Villeroy. Known as Mennecy porcelain, the factory was actually established in 1734 in Paris itself, in the rue de Charonne, and only moved out to Mennecy in 1748 under pressure from the specially favoured and royal factory at Vincennes. The products of Mennecy during the period when it was in the rue de Charonne to a large extent imitated St Cloud and Chantilly porcelains, though they always have a distinctive brilliantly glassy 'wet' glaze. Highly original in design, however, are the unique toilet-pots with covers modelled in the form of boars' heads (Plate 20). Fortunately the pair have survived in a perfect state in their contemporary leather case, tooled to resemble a number of slim novels. The mature, and often highly accomplished, Mennecy style of the following period was chiefly inspired by the royal Vincennes-Sèvres products, which form a totally different chapter in the history of European porcelain.

The Modeller's Period at Meissen, –c. 1735–55

The furnishing of the Japanese Palace in Dresden with magnificently painted porcelain had happily satisfied Augustus the Strong from 1720, but in 1729 he had the Japanese Palace enlarged to nearly twice its size and planned a chapel with porcelain reliefs on the walls, a pulpit and an altar of porcelain, even the organ-pipes were to be of porcelain! However, although attempts at porcelain figure sculpture were made as early as 1727, when Gottlieb Kirchner was appointed the first chief modeller, little was achieved until 1731–32, despite Augustus the Strong's eager desire to have the twelve nearly life-size figures of the apostles executed in porcelain for the chapel.

In 1731 the Elector engaged a young sculptor, Johann Joachim Kaendler (b. 1706), who was to replace Kirchner as *Modellmeister* two years later, a few months before Augustus the Strong died. In those two years he and Kirchner produced a number of the large-scale animals and birds in the white (Fig. 12) which were part of the grandiose scheme for the Japanese Palace, and, although this plan was not abandoned immediately after the death of Augustus the Strong, but was continued out of piety by the modellers as over-time until 1741, the energies and creative impulse of Kaendler soon took another form.

The true successor of Augustus the Strong in the patronage of the porcelain factory was not his son, but the new ambitious minister, Count von Brühl. As Director of Meissen from 1733 to 1763, von Brühl's personal taste and his conviction that Kaendler was a modeller of genius led the factory along new, stimulating, exciting, often extravagantly costly, paths, which were characterised by a degree of perfectionism matching the monumental splendour of the daring conceptions essayed. For the next twenty years the Meissen factory was without serious rivals in Europe, and, despite the most extravagant demands made upon the factory by Count von Brühl, Meissen's annual profits grew from 38,319 thalers in 1740 to 222,150 thalers in 1752. There were agents of the factory in thirty-two German cities, big depots in Warsaw, large trade orders with Paris, where it was fashionable to mount the porcelain in ormolu; in Russia the Czarina Elizabeth was a large buyer, whilst even in England 'Dresden china' was fast becoming the fashion.

Turning to the products of this period, the reader will find the quantity of work so enormous and so

Fig. 14

Harlequin with beer tankard, modelled by Kaendler in 1738. Meissen about 1740. Mark: crossed swords. Together with his other *Commedia dell'arte* figures, this harlequin ranks among Kaendler's finest creations in the medium of porcelain sculpture. Ht. 16.5 cm. ($6\frac{1}{2}$ in.).

bewilderingly varied that the danger of drowning in a sea of porcelain patterns, figures and giant services is very real. The great change of emphasis from the painted surface to the sculptured, modelled outline was established by about 1735 and continued throughout the period. The great table services, Count Sulkowsky's in 1735–36 and Count von Brühl's own 'Swan Service', 1737–41 (Fig. 13) are giant expressions of this change of taste. The painted decoration was restricted almost entirely to the coats of arms; the elaborate ornamentation of the individual vessels (tureens, plates, etc.) ranged from moulded scenes in low relief to the smothering of the surface in a riotous application of flowers, putti, shells, dolphins, rocks, tritons, clouds, swans, flames, nereids, nymphs and goddesses–all executed in the round. This was porcelain in the Baroque style at its most capricious, most fragile–and on a giant scale, never again to be equalled in porcelain.

Only in a visit to Dresden itself can this fantastic achievement in porcelain be appreciated, though now many of the most impressive have disappeared. No book can hope to illustrate adequately the magnificent porcelain creations of this great period of Meissen, which so impressed those at the Dresden court, such as the English ambassador Sir Charles Hanbury-Williams. In a letter from Dresden in 1748 he writes: 'I was once at a Dinner where we sat down at one table two hundred and six people ('twas at Count Brühl's). When the Desert was set on, I thought it was the most wonderful thing I ever beheld. I fancy'd myself either in a Garden or at an Opera, But I could not imagine that I was at Dinner. In the Middle of the Table was the Fountain of the

Piazza Navona at Rome, at least eight foot high, which ran all the while with rose-water and 'tis said that Piece alone cost six thousand Dollars'. This *tour de force* in white porcelain is no longer there to be marvelled at nor is the 'Temple of Honour', the famous centre-piece, made for Augustus III in 1748, but a few similar though rather smaller temples survive in Dresden and Germany and, oddly enough, one splendid but little known example in England, at Longleat (Plate 34).

For the most part, however, the reader will be able to enjoy the innumerable small independent figures. After 1730, the *chinoiserie* figures play a very minor part, for their place was quickly taken by the folk figures, partly inspired by the French engravings of Comte de Caylus, entitled 'Cris de Paris'. The most comprehensive set of these Meissen figures in

Plate 26
The Goddess Ki Mao Sao, made at Bow (London) about 1750. This group is ingeniously copied from the engraving by Aubert after the painting by Antoine Watteau (about 1719) entitled: 'Idole de la Déesse KI MAO SAO dans le Royaume de Mang au pays de Laos' (see Fig. 28) Ht. 18.0 cm. (7 in.). *British Museum, London.*

Plate 27
Lady in a crinoline inspecting the wares of the trinket-seller. Modelled at Meissen, probably by Kaendler about 1745. Ht. 17.1 cm. (6¾ in.). *British Museum, London.*

England can now be seen in Lord Fisher's collection at the Fitzwilliam Museum, Cambridge. With their rhythmical movements, their bold modelling and simple vivid colouring, emphasising the dazzling whiteness of the porcelain, these 'Cris de Paris' figures demonstrate just how agreeable Kaendler's talents were. The set of Miners is in the same vein, but with the figures of characters from the *Commedia dell'arte*, the Harlequins, the Mezzetinos and the Columbines, there is a new violent, gymnastic movement, a bizarre ribaldry and an almost uncontrolled mêlée of clashing colours (Fig. 14).

Kaendler's great innovation was to model figure-groups satirising contemporary life, court personages, costume, etc. Rarely did anyone but Kaendler produce in this category a group of equal merit to the Crinoline Lady in the British Museum (Plate 27). It is to this *genre* that Meissen's vast array of 'Lovers', 'Dresden shepherdesses', 'Musicians' and 'Gardeners' belong, and by 1740 they began to take the public's fancy and for the next fifteen years formed the bulk of the factory's output. But for many the beautifully coloured, small figures of birds and animals, which Kaendler made in the early days (*c.* 1735), remain the most enjoyable. Kaendler found most of the world's animals and birds in Augustus' aviaries and parks at Moritzburg and, modelling from nature, he created some of the most naturalistic glimpses of animals ever expressed in sculpture (Plate 25).

Kaendler's style was essentially Baroque in its use of dramatic movement combined with strong masses, its blending of turbulent energy with disciplined symmetry. But in Paris there was born a new style of graceful movement, of freedom from symmetrical harmony, of soft colours and slender airy delicacy of form, the Rococo. But whereas the French Rococo remained restrained and elegant, the new style which swept through Germany built up into a crescendo of wild extravagances lasting into the 1770s, long after the *Louis Seize* style had restored a new symmetry to French art. Beginning in Nymphenburg and Würzburg about 1745 and ending in the 'Potsdam Rococo' of Frederick the

Great, the German Rococo was completely whole-hearted and all-embracing.

At Meissen, Kaendler's dominant position held the Rococo at bay, but in 1748 the appointment of a new and very gifted modeller, Friedrich Elias Meyer, only twenty-four years old, introduced into Meissen a new breath of artistic life. Kaendler's own visit to Paris in 1749 may have tipped the scales, for after 1750 the Meissen figure style changed. The strong colours disappeared and a pale yellow and a soft mauve were preferred. The figures were placed on bases with moulded Rococo scrollwork. Meyer's slender figures turning about with graceful gestures replaced the vital heroic forms of Kaendler.

But at heart Kaendler, and hence Meissen, remained imbued with the spirit of the Baroque; consequently, the products of Meissen after 1750 were not in tune with the spirit of the decade, the Rococo, and it was no longer at Meissen that porcelain found its most expressive creative form. There was a falling-off in ideas and workmanship after 1750; the production of figures seems to have been little more than a commercial enterprise. When the blow was struck by Prussia's army victoriously occupying Dresden in September, 1756, it seems almost to have been a *coup de grâce* for the Meissen factory. Meissen never recovered from the paralysing effect of the Seven Years' War, for in Europe the supremacy was usurped by Sèvres, and in Germany many new factories sprang up to give expression to German Rococo in porcelain.

The French Rise to Supremacy

The National Manufactory of porcelain in France, which alone among the French porcelain factories was to play a dominant European role, began in a disused royal château at Vincennes, close to Paris, in 1738, but for seven years had little success. Eventually in 1745 a company was formed (with the king subscribing a large proportion of the capital, largely because of Madame de Pompadour's great interest in it) and was granted several important privileges, including the exclusive right to make 'porcelain in Saxon manner, that is to say, painted and gilded with human figures'. From the outset, the avowed intention was to rival Meissen porcelain, so envious were the French of Dresden's great success. From 1753, the factory was formally known as 'Manufacture royale de porcelaine' and for the first time the mark of the crossed 'L's'– the royal cipher – was announced as the factory mark, and date-letters for each year were commenced. This decree of 1753 marks the end of the first period of the factory, during which tremendous progress had been made.

The very earliest Vincennes porcelain has never been reliably identified. It was unmarked, but may be presumed to resemble Chantilly in some respects, since the workmen came from there, and because Bachelier states that before his appointment in 1748

Fig. 15

Bouquet of soft-paste porcelain flowers painted in colours. Vincennes; 1749. This monumental bouquet, a masterpiece of technical skill, consists of no less than 480 flowers of various kinds mounted on metal and was presented in 1749 by the Dauphine of France to her father, Augustus III, King of Poland and Elector of Saxony. The flowers are arranged in a vase of plain white glazed porcelain, decorated with relief sprays and framed by two white glazed porcelain groups symbolising the Arts, modelled by Depierreux. The *rocaille* gilt-bronze base is by Jean-Claude Duplessis. Ht. 115.0 cm. (45½ in.). *Der Zwinger, Dresden.*

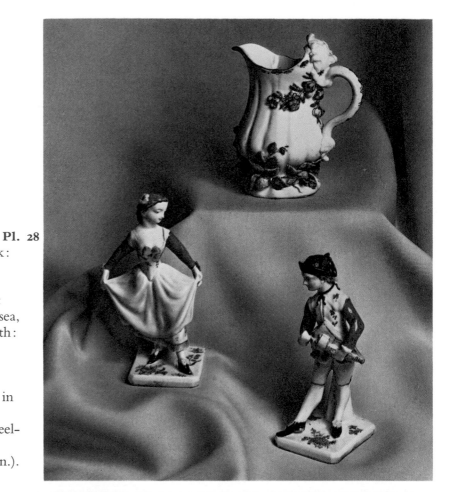

Plate 28 Pl. 28
Milk-jug, made at Chelsea about 1745–8. Mark: incised triangle. Ht. 13.5 cm. (5¼ in.). Pair of figures, the girl dancing to the music of the hurdy-gurdy played by the youth. Made about 1751–3 at the break-away rival factory in Chelsea, known as the 'Girl-in-the-Swing' factory. Youth: Ht. 14.9 cm. (5⅞ in.). *British Museum, London.*

Plate 29
Scent-bottle, made at Benjamin Lund's factory in Bristol about 1750. Copied from the contemporary Bristol glass scent-bottles with their wheel-cut, faceted surfaces. Ht. 7.5 cm. (3 in.). Swan, made at Lowestoft about 1780. Ht. 6.5 cm. (2½ in.). *Both in the British Museum, London.*

Pl. 29

46

Plate 30
Pantalon, a character from the Italian Comedy, made at Fürstenberg about 1755 from a model by Simon Feilner. Ht. 19.4 cm. (7⅝ in.). *Victoria and Albert Museum, London.*

Plate 31
Scaramouche and Columbine, two characters from the Italian Comedy, made at Wilhelm Kaspar Wegely's factory in Berlin between 1751 and 1757. Mark: w (in underglaze blue). The use of a chocolate-brown for Scaramouche's jacket and breeches is quite exceptional not only at the Wegely factory but on European porcelain in general. Ht. 17.1 cm. (6¾ in.). *British Museum, London.*

Pl. 30

Pl. 31

the decoration was only a 'crude imitation of the Japanese'.

As early as 1749, porcelain of sufficiently high quality was produced to stand the supreme test; a bouquet of no less than 480 enamelled porcelain blooms was sent by the Dauphine Marie-Josephe to her father, Augustus III, in Dresden, where it still remains (Fig. 15). This colourful bouquet was mounted in ormolu with a glazed white vase and two glazed white groups—none was enamelled. In Dresden this new French soft-paste porcelain must have received the most critical scrutiny beside the hard-paste of Meissen.

Certainly, enamelled figures in the manner of Meissen were attempted at Vincennes in the first period before 1753, but very few have survived (Plate 24), most being plain white-glazed groups. By 1753, the factory had broken away from the 'Dresden china figure' tradition by making unglazed 'biscuit' porcelain figures in a misguided imitation of marble (Fig. 16). This rejection of glaze meant the total loss of colour, which was, however, to be of fashionable popularity when the classical revival dominated France from about 1760 until the end of the century. These figures were a far cry from Kaendler's sculpture at Meissen. The harsh satire of folk subjects of Meissen disappeared before a host of pastoral and mythological scenes, largely influenced

48

by the overwhelming genius of François Boucher.

In the realm of tableware, Vincennes's simple forms (Fig. 17), some graceful, but many quite crude, gave way to the subdued scrolled or shell motif of the French Rococo or to the more elaborate exotic designs, like the well-known *vaisseau-à-mât* (Fig. 18). One of the earliest of these ambitious pieces is the vase-candelabra with the elephant motif in the Wallace Collection at Hertford House; it is dated 1756 (Plate 37). These designs owe nothing to Meissen; they are utterly French.

The year 1756 was a year of triumph for the French royal factory. The factory moved from Vincennes to Sèvres into the larger premises which

Fig. 16
Figure group, *The Grape Eaters*, in soft-paste biscuit porcelain. Vincennes or Sèvres; about 1755. Mark: 'B', incised. The original model is ascribed to Boucher and is one of those most frequently reproduced in later times. Ht. 24.1 cm. (9½ in.). *Musée National de Céramique, Sèvres.*

Fig. 17
Vase with enamelled flower decoration. Mark: interlaced 'L's enclosing a dot (painted in blue over-glaze). Vincennes, about 1745–50. Ht. 12.1 cm. (4¾ in.). *British Museum, London.*

had been specially built there so that it might be near to Madame de Pompadour's new château at Bellevue. There was even a summer house for the king at the factory. In the same year the great rival, Meissen, fell to Frederick the Great, and for the length of the Seven Years' War Meissen was out of the running; her best men in exile, her kilns and ovens destroyed rather than fall into the hands of the Prussians, Sèvres was left a clear field. Rapidly the lead was taken by Sèvres, until the Sèvres styles and new achievements were copied in every European country, even finally at Meissen.

One of the great changes at Sèvres was the shedding of the light 'Vincennes' style of painting on the tablewares (Fig. 17) for laborious overall colouring that left no particle of the porcelain bare to the eye (Plate 42). The central panels would be painted like an oil painting in miniature, with every effort and every detail as if it were an important canvas. The factory employed men like Veillard, Asselin and gifted younger men like Chabry fils, Morin and Dodin, to execute these panels. Most characteristic of the Sèvres style is the surrounding of these 'panel-pictures' with a ground colour. At Vincennes they invented a deep, but uneven, blue, known as *bleu lapis*, which was an underglaze colour (Fig. 19). It was much copied at the English factories of Chelsea and Derby where it was called 'Mazarine blue' (Plate 44). This pulsating rich lustrous *bleu lapis* was replaced in 1763 with a strong deep blue enamel called *bleu-de-roi* or more correctly, *bleu nouveau* (Plate 52). So technically perfect, so even and powerfully opaque, the excellence of this brilliant ground colour seems to us today mechanical—

Plate 32
The Tiger and the Bamboo Pattern:
the Japanese original LEFT was made at Arita, with enamels in Kakiemon style, about 1700; the Chelsea version RIGHT was made about 1755 and bears the mark: an anchor in red. Diam. 19.5 cm. ($7\frac{3}{4}$ in.). (Japanese); width 20.5 cm. ($8\frac{1}{8}$ in.). (Chelsea). *British Museum, London.*

Plate 33
Vase with a Bacchus and attendants, made at Capodimonte (near Naples) about 1750. Mark: a blue fleur-de-lis. Ht. 26.7 cm. ($10\frac{1}{2}$ in.). *Victoria and Albert Museum, London.*

51

Fig. 19

almost to a fault. Not so at the struggling Meissen factory, where its secret was enviously sought, even to the point of sending members of their staff to Paris in 1766, specially charged with discovering the secret.

The same process of transforming the uneven *bleu céleste* (turquoise), the *jaune jonquille* (yellow) and the green into a ground colour of unequalled smoothness was successfully carried out in the sixties. The one ground colour that was not altered was the pink, the *rose Pompadour*, as it has been called in England since the mid-1760s. It was only invented in 1757 but is rarely found outside the decade 1757–67. There was also a taste at Sèvres in the sixties for applying patterns (diapers, networks, pebbled or vermicule marbling) in gold over the ground colour, but by the 1780s the so-called 'jewelling' was invented by Cotteau, by which a blob of coloured enamel is fused over a dot of gold or silver

Fig. 18

Pot-pourri vase in the shape of a single masted ship in soft-paste porcelain with polychrome and gold decoration. Sèvres, 1758. The design is said to derive from the ship on the coat-of-arms of the City of Paris and is quite unlike anything previously produced. To fire in fragile soft-paste porcelain these elaborately pierced vessels is proof of the technical skill achieved at Sèvres before 1760 but it is perhaps significant that only fourteen of these celebrated '*vaisseau à mât*' vases are known to have been sold from the factory. Ht. 43.9 cm. (17¼ in.). *Wallace Collection, London.*

Fig. 19

Covered vase, with *bleu lapis* and gilded decoration. Mark: Interlaced 'L's enclosing a dot (in gold). Vincennes, about 1750. Ht. 23.5 cm. (9¾ in.). *British Museum, London.*

Pl. 35

Plate 34
Temple of Minerva, a centre-piece made at
Meissen about 1745–50. Ht. 114.3 cm. (3 ft. 9 in.)
(from base of porcelain columns). Width 76.2 cm.
(2 ft. 6 in.). Depth. 52.0 cm. (1 ft. 8½ in.).
Collection of Marquis of Bath.

Plate 35
The so-called 'Maypole Dancers', an unusually
ambitious group, probably modelled by Joseph
Willems of Tournai; made at Chelsea about 1755.
Mark: red anchor. Ht. 35.5 cm. (14 in.).
Fitzwilliam Museum, Cambridge.

foil on to the ground colour (Plate 52).

Despite the warm beauty of the soft-paste porcelain produced at Sèvres, the desire to make a true hard-paste body remained unquenchable. Eventually in 1768, a French supply of kaolin was discovered near Limoges, and the first French hard-paste porcelain was produced the next year. But its production on a commercial scale only dates from 1772, by which time there were several other successful hard-paste factories in France, Paul Hannong's at Vaux, one in the Faubourg St Denis in Paris and at Limoges itself. The hard-paste porcelain at Sèvres never achieved any European importance, although the rare examples with a black ground, on which *chinoiserie* decoration is executed in platinum and gold (Fig. 20), are particularly dramatic – and testifies to the exceptionally early use of platinum for artistic purposes.

Fig. 20
Plate of hard-paste porcelain, with black ground colour and decoration in gold and platinum. Mark: '*Sèvres. X.*' (in red). Made at Sèvres about 1800. Diam. 24.4 cm. (9⅝ in.). *British Museum, London.*

Fig. 21
Virgin and Child; made at Limbach, about 1770. Ht. 28.7 cm. (11¼ in.). *British Museum, London.*

Plate 36
Covered vase encrusted with flowers, made at
Longton Hall (Staffordshire) about 1755. Ht.
37.5 cm. (14¾ in.). *British Museum, London.*

Plate 37
Candelabrum-vase 'à éléphants', designed most
probably by Jean-Claude Duplessis (working
1747–74). Mark: interlaced Ls containing the date
letter, D, (for 1756). Made at Sèvres in 1756.
Ht. 38.0 cm. (15 in.). *Wallace Collection, London.*

The Rest of Europe

German Porcelain after the Eclipse of Meissen

Apart from the porcelain factory in Vienna, which was never a serious rival, Meissen's monopoly had been unchallenged in Germany for forty years (1713–53). In Venice and in France, there were the local efforts to produce porcelain, but none succeeded in equalling the masterly achievements of Meissen and in no way competed with Meissen for the European market. With the change in style from Baroque to Rococo in the late forties in Germany, Meissen began to get out of step with current taste, and with the disruption of the Meissen factory during the Seven Years' War (1756–63), the new German porcelain factories had their opportunity. In Germany these young porcelain factories all owed their existence to court patronage, and it was at the Bavarian court in the grounds of the Nymphenburg Palace, near Munich, that European porcelain reached a new peak of delight in the new mode of expression, the Rococo.

Nymphenburg porcelain figures modelled by Franz Anton Bustelli are as desirable as anything created by Kaendler (Plate 38); indeed, only with the arrival of Bustelli at Nymphenburg in 1754 did the factory rise to greatness. This was the year when Graf Sigmund von Haimhausen, the moving spirit behind the factory, persuaded the Duke of Bavaria to give the porcelain venture official status. Since 1747, when Maria Anna Sophia, grand-daughter of Augustus the Strong, married the Elector, there had been a strong interest in the prospect of making porcelain, but without much success, although the actual secret of making porcelain seems to have been acquired from Vienna. Now, with Bustelli creating a new style of porcelain figures, a slim, graceful, elegant style, alive with movement, both spontaneous and yet exaggerated, theatrical yet highly refined, Nymphenburg porcelain became famous.

Bustelli himself, however, remains something of a mystery. Born at Locarno in 1723, the son of a bell-maker, he appears at Nymphenburg an accomplished modeller, whose most distinctive style has not been traced elsewhere. By 1760 he had developed his Rococo style to its logical conclusion, incorporating his fluid figures into the swirling lilting movement of his composition, so that the whole forms a unified composition of curving lines soaring laughingly to a frothy apex. His sixteen figures from the Italian *Commedia dell'arte* are among the greatest porcelain series ever designed. Much of his time was undoubtedly occupied modelling Rococo tablewares, for which the factory was justly famed. Although Nymphenburg porcelain continued to maintain a high standard and even achieves some remarkable new effects under Auliczek, the premature death of Bustelli in 1764 was a sad blow.

Other porcelain factories springing up at the various courts of the German princes expressed themselves in the Rococo style, too, though with less success, for none could boast a modeller as creative as Bustelli. However, the playfully absurd *chinoiserie* follies created by the French artists were re-interpreted by the German porcelain modellers, resulting in many delightful groups during the sixties, such as those of the anonymous *Chinesenmeister* who worked at the Elector of Mainz's factory at Höchst.

The Höchst factory, which also acquired the secret of porcelain-making from Vienna through the potter Ringler, began producing fair quality porcelain *c.* 1750–53; later it attracted a modeller called Johann Peter Melchior (1767–79) whose distinctive style foreshadows the oversweet charm of typical nineteenth-century 'china groups'. His work, largely ignoring the *chinoiserie*, concentrates on that other passion of the Rococo, the pastoral (Plate 39). His numerous models of children are especially charming and spontaneous, but the idyllic emphasis in his adult figures becomes monotonous. The technical perfection of the glaze, combined with a particularly striking rose-pink flesh colour for the skin, a strong green for the grassy mounds on which his figures are usually placed and a good colour sense redeem many of his rather boring subjects.

The Elector Palatine, Karl Theodor von der Pfalz, also fell a victim to the porcelain craze, and in 1755 granted an eminent French faience manufacturer, Paul-Anton Hannong, the most favourable terms for starting a porcelain manufactory in the Palatine at Frankenthal. Hannong had been forced to go beyond the frontiers of France by Louis XV's decree in 1754 protecting the monopoly of the Royal Vin-

Fig. 22
Pietà, a semi-'hard-paste' glazed porcelain. Doccia
factory about 1770. The rock beneath the figure
of Christ bears the incised inscription: ECCE
QVOMODO MORITVR IVSTUS ET NEMO PERCIPIT
CORDE, attributed to Massimiliano Soldani-Benzi
(1657–1740), some of whose models were
acquired by Ginori. Ht. 27.8 cm. (11 in.). *British
Museum, London.*

Plate 38
Sleeper awakened; modelled by Franz Anton Bustelli at Nymphenburg (near Munich) about 1760. Mark: 2 shields. Ht. 24.1 cm. (9½ in.). *Cecil Higgins Museum, Bedford.*

Plate 39
The Sleeping Shepherdess, modelled by Johann
Peter Melchior at Höchst (near Frankfurt) about
1770. Mark: a wheel (in blue). Ht. 21.5 cm.
(8½ in.). *British Museum, London.*

cennes factory; the Elector Palatine was a very lucky beneficiary. But Hannong also owed his success in part to the aid of the Viennese, Ringler, who had left Höchst to work at Strasbourg in 1753, where their successful Strasbourg hard-paste porcelain roused the French authorities to protect Vincennes. Frankenthal is particularly noted for its fine figure modelling, and among the several highly gifted modellers employed at the factory was Karl Gottlieb Lück, whose work is of unusual fine quality. He was extremely versatile, creating elaborate *chinoiseries* (Plate 47), satirical comments on contemporary society, as well as hunting groups and the more routine figures in the porcelain repertoire. Frankenthal tablewares were also of extremely good quality, painted in a good palette, frequently with figure-

Fig. 23
Detail of the 'Porcelain-Room' erected in the Royal Villa at Portici, near Naples, between 1757–9. About 3,000 interlocking porcelain plaques cover the walls; modelled by Giuseppe and Stefano Gricci; painted by J. S. Fischer and Luigi Restile; made at the Capodimonte factory. 5.5 × 4.3 × 4.3 m. (18 × 14 × 14 ft.).

Fig. 24
View of the 'Porcelain-Room' erected in the palace of Aranjuez, south of Madrid, between 1763–5. Modelled by Giuseppe Gricci. The raw materials for the porcelain were probably imported from Naples. Made at the Buen Retiro factory, on the outskirts of Madrid.

subjects. By the end of the eighteenth century, the impetus was gone, and when the French occupied the town in 1794 it was in effect the end of the porcelain factory.

Another German prince who spent enormous sums of money in an attempt to have his own porcelain manufactory was Karl I, the Duke of Brunswick. Established in the old castle at Fürstenberg, the embryonic factory experimented without success for six years until the Viennese porcelain potter, Benckgraff, was induced by promises of great rewards to come to the rescue. From 1753 true porcelain was made, and with the aid of modellers, like Simon Feilner, figures of originality and energy were produced, though the Seven Years' War adversely affected the factory's progress. But from

1770 to 1790 the factory was most competently run and produced some remarkably expressive figure-groups, though many of them are little more than variants of Meissen or Nymphenburg models (Plate 30). The factory secured the patronage of Jérôme Bonaparte and his consort during the French occupation, and so prospered. The factory is still in existence and, like the Nymphenburg factory, has reproduced many of its old models.

The Dukedom of Würtemberg was more unfortunate than the German principalities so far mentioned, because it alone had no local supply of china-clay. At great expense, the Duke Carl Eugen had the clay brought from Passau and enlisted the skill of the Viennese potter Ringler, in 1759. So satisfactory were the terms, that the wandering Ringler settled

Plate 40
Pair of mugs, made and painted at the Worcester
China Works with the arms of the City of
Worcester by James Rogers in 1757 for the City
Corporation. Ht. 27.9 cm. (11 in.). *City of
Worcester Corporation.*

Plate 41
Mug, painted with a 'chinoiserie' scene; made at
Liverpool about 1765. Ht. 16.0 cm. (6¼ in.).
Tankard, with a transfer-printed portrait of
Queen Charlotte, consort of George III, by John
Sadler; made at Liverpool about 1760. Ht.
14.5 cm. (5¾ in.). Transfer-printing on porcelain
was singularly popular in England, especially at
Worcester, Caughley and Liverpool in the second
half of eighteenth century. *Both in the British
Museum, London.*

Fig. 25
Portrait medallion with incised signature (on the reverse): *Fortunato Tolerazzi Fece Venesia 1763* and marked (on the front) 'v' in relief. Made in Venice at the factory established by Nathaniel Friedrich Hewelcke and his wife, Maria Dorothea, in 1758 after they had fled from Dresden following upon its occupation by the army of Frederick the Great of Prussia during the Seven Years' War. Ht. 22.9 cm. (9 in.). (without frame). *British Museum, London.*

Fig. 26
Ice-cream cup, soft-paste porcelain of ivory tone, painted in enamel colours. Mark: incised on base: 'мв'. Marieberg (Sweden); about 1766–9. Pierre Berthevin, who had worked at Mennecy, took over the managership of the Marieberg factory in 1766, and succeeded in making soft-paste porcelain there. These little 'cream-cups' or 'jelly-pots' – and between 1772–1788 about 15,000 of them were made at Marieberg – reveal the strong influence of Mennecy in the paste, shape and enamel-painting. Ht. 8.3 cm. (3¼ in.). *British Museum, London.*

down in Würtemberg at Ludwigsburg, where the factory was established by the duke. The ducal enthusiasm for porcelain was such that in 1777 the duke himself visited the Sèvres and Wedgwood factories.

Ludwigsburg porcelain is markedly inferior to most German porcelain, for the paste is less white and the glaze imperfect and irregular; but the paste was much more plastic, enabling the modellers to achieve far more complicated figure sculpture in porcelain on a much larger scale (Plate 48). Thus, smaller versions of the large stone sculptures of Domenico Ferretti, the court sculptor, were made in porcelain. The duke was particularly fond of porcelain figures and was justly pleased with the many new creations; but the porcelain was never really suitable for tablewares, and consequently, although excellently painted, the forms lack originality, for all the best talent was concentrated on the figure-work.

Before discussing the only other really large-scale porcelain factory in eighteenth-century Germany, the Prussian court factory in Berlin, some brief mention must be made of some of the odd score of minor German porcelain factories, whose existence was frequently short-lived but whose productions were often incredibly accomplished. The resources of the Prince-Bishops of Fulda, for example, were not very considerable, but it was under the patron-age of the Prince-Bishop Heinrich von Bibra that this tiny capital commenced a porcelain factory in 1764. After three years it was totally destroyed by fire, but within a year it was back in production, and in the seventies created Rococo figures of exceptional merit, made of the highest quality porcelain and decorated with the most delicate painting (Plate 46). The tablewares are also of high quality, but even at this late date they were mainly copied from Meissen designs.

The more wealthy Prince-Bishops of Würzburg, whose eighteenth-century *Residenz* palace, with ceilings painted by Tiepolo, is one of the most delightful manifestations of the Rococo, also encouraged a porcelain factory, though it seems to have lasted for little more than five years, from 1775 to 1780. Nevertheless, its tablewares often have a distinctive quality which has a curious charm (Plate 43). The attribution of some figures to this factory has recently been firmly established, but they appear to be of relatively poor quality.

Many more German princelings had porcelain factories of good quality, but, lacking a strong character of their own, the products are usually echoes of Meissen figures and Berlin table-wares. The forests and clay seams of Thuringia gave rise to a host of small factories in the latter part of the eighteenth century, many of which still survive. A large number of their products are only of average

Plate 42
Tray with open-work sides, painted with two
lovers and a Peeping Tom. Made at Sèvres in
1766, and painted by Chabry fils. Width 24.0 cm.
(9½ in.). *British Museum, London.*

Plate 43
Coffee-pot, with dragon handle; made at
Würzburg about 1775. Ht. 21.5 cm. (8½ in.). Vase,
made at Louis Fournier's factory in Copenhagen
between 1759 and 1766. Mark: F5 (in gold).
Ht. 15.9 cm. (6¼ in.). *Both in the British Museum,
London.*

Fig. 27
'Goat and Bee' jug inscribed 'Chelsea, 1745' with
the incised triangle mark on the base. Made at
Chelsea in 1745. This date, 1745, is the earliest yet
found on any English porcelain. Ht. 10.9 cm.
(4¼ in.). *British Museum, London.*

quality, but some, especially the figures of Limbach (Fig. 21), have a simple charm that is true of much peasant or folk art.

How different was the story of porcelain in that growing German power, Prussia. Frederick the Great had, for more than a decade, been most eager to have his own porcelain factory, but it was 1752 before porcelain was made in Berlin, by a merchant called Wegely, under the patronage of the king. Wegely's porcelain, however, was not good enough for the king, and when Wegely was not allowed by Frederick to have Meissen's secrets after Dresden had fallen to the Prussian army in 1756, Wegely abandoned his porcelain venture. Wegely's porcelain is scarce, and much that survives is figure-work of an original design, probably the work of Ernst Heinrich Reichard (Plate 31). Little of it is enamelled because of the technical difficulties, which Wegely never succeeded in overcoming with complete certainty.

Frederick's court was kept well supplied by Meissen during the war, but it was Frederick the Great's intention to have his own factory of equal merit in Berlin, and a new royal factory was started in Berlin in 1761 by Gotzkowsky, with the help of Meissen workmen and having many royal privileges and favourable concessions. Despite these advantages, Berlin failed to take the place of Meissen, for the European leadership had already passed to the French royal factory at Sèvres. The discovery of clay deposits at Brachwitz near Halle resulted in a cold bluish tinge, which characterises the greater part of Berlin porcelain that survives.

The factory was most famous for its table-services, and it was not until 1790 that the factory succeeded in attracting a good *Modellmeister*, Johann Carl Friedrich Riese. Riese did excellent work in the neo-classical style in biscuit porcelain; he collaborated successfully with the court architect, Genelli, who was also a modeller, and with another called Schadow, who was responsible in 1818 for the table-centre and other appointments presented to the Duke of Wellington by his Prussian allies. A splendid example of their combined work can be seen in the Temple of Bacchus (Plate 55), with its biscuit figure set in a pseudo-classical structure. The Temple contrasts strikingly with Kaendler's Temple of Minerva (Plate 34), that Baroque conception diluted with mild concessions to the Rococo. Here in Berlin the Meissen tradition of great table-services with splendid centre-pieces was continued long after the fashion had changed elsewhere in Europe; but when contrasted with the Meissen Baroque conception these later Berlin productions become glaringly inadequate, and this icing-sugar misuse of porcelain no longer satisfies. In the presence of such productions the desire to escape from the mock marble porcelain and to be back with the true mid-eighteenth-century feeling for porcelain is compelling.

Peripheral Areas of Manufacture in Europe

The German states were, therefore the great centre of true hard-paste porcelain manufacture throughout the eighteenth century, whilst France was the leading country in the production of soft-paste, or artificial porcelain. By the time that the smaller German states were beginning to make their own porcelain (about 1750-55) a number of other European countries had also started their own porcelain factories.

In Italy, after the Vezzi factory in Venice had closed in 1727, there was a gap of only ten years before an attempt was again made to produce porcelain – this time at Doccia, near Florence. Tuscany passed by treaty in 1737 to the husband of Maria Theresa, Francis III of Lorraine, who later became Emperor of Austria. The Marchese Carlo Ginori of Florence was the leading political figure in Tuscany, and by his aptitude and astuteness at the Imperial Court in Vienna, he retained a position of great consequence in central Italy. During a visit to Vienna in 1737, Carlo Ginori engaged the services of Johann Karl Wendelin Anreiter von Zirnfeld, a particularly gifted painter of porcelain, who settled at Doccia with his son for ten years. Some, as yet anonymous, potter from the Du Paquier factory in Vienna seems to have brought the secret of manufacture to Doccia. By 1740 sufficient progress had been made to send sample specimens to the court at Vienna, but commercial sales do not seem to have started until 1746 – in fact, no sooner than in most other European countries.

The Doccia porcelain is a hybrid, rather than a true, hard-paste, more easily distinguished than most porcelain by its markedly grey appearance and sticky, smeared glaze, which does not hide the rough quality of the body. The earliest products were tablewares with decoration in blue only (Plate 21). Some of the more ambitious have double walls in the manner of the Fukien *blanc-de-chine* porcelain, in which the outer wall is pierced and decorated in relief. The more usual vessels of this early period (c. 1745) are in the Baroque style, often painted in greyish blue by means of stencils – a practice used in no other European porcelain factory of the eighteenth century.

The Marchese Carlo Ginori, who died in 1757, and his successor, Lorenzo Ginori, clearly hoped, as had Augustus the Strong at Meissen, to produce large-scale sculpture in porcelain. Some remarkable Baroque figures, over 2 ft. 6 in. high, survive, to testify to the successful determination of the factory in the years 1770-75. These works are impressive, not only for the tremendous demands they inflict on the material, but also for their sculptural force and powerful expression (Fig. 22). The factory, which still survives today, produced a wealth of smaller figures, many of which are enamelled and, of course, a great quantity of fine table-ware, the large vases

Plate 44
Toilet-box, heart-shaped, with two Cupids
garlanding a lamb as a knop; made at Chelsea
about 1760–5. L. 12.1 cm. (4¾ in.). Covered pot,
made at Chelsea about 1760–5. Mark: a gold
anchor. Ht. 15.2 cm. (6 in.). This dark blue,
known at Chelsea as 'marzarine blue', was in
imitation of the Sèvres 'bleu lapis'. *British Museum,
London.*

Plate 45
Clio, the Muse of History, modelled at Derby
about 1760 from the engraving by J. Daullé after
the painting by François Boucher. Ht. 22.9 cm.
(9 in.). *British Museum, London.*

and centre-pieces of which are conceived in the same sculptural spirit.

The year after the Marchese Carlo Ginori had brought Anreiter back with him from Vienna to Doccia, Maria Amalia Christiana, a daughter of Augustus the Strong of Saxony, was married to Charles of Bourbon, King of Naples and Sicily. As part of her dowry she brought with her in 1738 to the court of Naples seventeen porcelain table-services – all from Meissen. Charles was quickly infected and in 1743 started a factory in the grounds of the Capodimonte Palace, just north of Naples. Charles would not leave behind his favourite hobby when in 1759 he was called back to Spain to succeed his half-brother as King of Spain. The transplanting of the Capodimonte factory 'lock, stock and barrel' to the Buen Retiro palace in Madrid proved a failure, because, although it continued until 1808, nothing original or creative grew up to take the place of the strong Capodimonte character, which could not survive for more than a few years in Spain.

Capodimonte porcelain, which is a most translucent soft-paste, began by copying the Meissen porcelain of the period 1730–40. The imitations (Plate 33) are unmistakably Italian in palette and decoration, for the colours are usually stippled on, or, in the case of flowers, drawn with the finest hair lines. The dominant pale orange-red combined with green, grey and brown gives a subdued harmony to the factory decoration. The love of clouds painted in violet and that same pale orange-red is present on most pieces.

The Capodimonte factory was, however, swept into the Rococo tidal wave and produced one of the finest and most exciting creations both of porcelain and of Rococo art – the 'porcelain-room' in the Royal Villa at Portici (Fig. 23). In the two years 1757–59, a room $18 \times 14 \times 14$ feet, with only five large mirrors and one door, was entirely covered with porcelain. The white porcelain 'silhouetted' the gilded Rococo scrolls and the brightly enamelled *chinoiserie* figures, flowers and swans executed separately in porcelain in high relief. Only by visiting this room can anyone realise how perfect porcelain can be as a decorative medium when applied on this comprehensive and magnificent scale.

A repetition of this masterpiece was achieved in 1763–65 by the factory in its Spanish home at Buen Retiro for the Palace of Aranjuez, south of Madrid (Fig. 24). Another 'porcelain-room', executed ten years later in the Royal Palace at Madrid in the neo-classical style, demonstrates the decline of the factory at Buen Retiro. The porcelain is no longer a brilliant white, having a strong yellow tinge, and the glassy glaze is cracked and uneven. The cold colour scheme of gold and turquoise is limited and harsh, lacking all the gay exuberance of the two earlier rooms.

After Charles of Naples took the Capodimonte factory with him to Spain in 1759, there was a gap of twelve years before his son resurrected the idea of a Neapolitan porcelain factory. The new Naples royal factory produced a glassy soft-paste, but it was little more than an echo of Capodimonte's greatness. Only under the directorship of Domenico Veduti did the factory rise to importance. The change of taste to a neo-classical style immediately became evident, and the factory took the lead in the production of services with classical subjects, the 'Herculaneum' service sent to Spain in 1781 and the 'Etruscan' service sent to England in 1785.

There were several other Italian porcelain factories in the second half of the eighteenth century, mainly in or around Venice (Fig. 25), but their grey hard-paste body covered with a wet-looking glaze is never comparable to the beauty of the Capodimonte.

An extreme example of this peripheral manifestation of the European mania for porcelain occurred on the north side of the Alps, at Zürich, in 1763. For two years only the Zürich factory produced soft-paste porcelain; then kaolin from Lorraine enabled the factory to produce some of the most beautiful European tableware in porcelain, for the smoky greenish glaze is a sympathetic ground for the fine enamel painting of Swiss landscapes. The tablewares, though substantially built, are beautifully finished (Plate 49). The figures are mainly echoes of the Ludwigsburg factory, from whence the modeller came to Zürich.

In the north of Europe, the Danish royal court attracted the runaway Christoph Konrad Hunger, whose return to Meissen after the Vezzi factory in Venice had foundered in 1727 was not a success. Hunger was definitely in Copenhagen in 1730 and in 1737, but his attempts to found a porcelain factory were again a failure. In 1754 an Irishman, Daniel MacCarthy, made porcelain in Copenhagen, as is proved by the medallion of King Frederick V in the Rosenborg Castle, inscribed: GOD BLESS YOUR MAYES. AND I WISH YOU A HAPPY NEW YR. 17 DMC 54. Little else survives to show the extent of his productions, though the records show that a Meissen painter, J. G. Mehlhorn, was there from 1754. Only with the arrival of Louis Fournier from Sèvres in 1759 did the Copenhagen factory really begin to produce porcelain on a commercial scale. Fournier's porcelain was a beautiful soft-paste type that was frequently marred by defects in enamelling and glaze. This extremely rare porcelain is in the French style, and one of the largest and finest examples is the vase in the British Museum (Plate 43). However, so high were the costs of his productions that in 1765 he was commanded to close the factory. Kaolin had been found on the island of Bornholm in 1755, but it was not until the year 1771 that a hard-paste porcelain was made in Copenhagen.

Pierre Berthevin, who had come from the Mennecy factory to Fournier's factory, went further north in 1765 and joined the Swedish faience factory

Fig. 28
Engraving by Aubert after Antoine Watteau's
painting (about 1719), entitled: *Idole de la Déesse
KI MAO SAO dans le Royaume de Mang au pays
de Laos*. The Bow (London) porcelain factory
created a figure group in 1750–2 based on this
engraving – see Plate 26. *British Museum, London*.

Plate 46
'Le Panier Mystérieux', made at Fulda about 1770, perhaps modelled by Laurentius Russinger from the engraving by René Gaillard after the painting by François Boucher. Mark: a cross (in underglaze blue). Ht. 21.5 cm. (8½ in.). *British Museum, London.*

Plate 47
A Chinese pavilion, modelled by Karl Gottlieb Lück at Frankenthal about 1770. Mark: a crowned CT (monogram) in underglaze blue. Ht. 25.5 cm. (10 in.). *British Museum, London.*

Pl. 46

I. 47

at Marieberg, near Stockholm, where in 1766 he was able to commence the first Swedish porcelain factory. The products were, of course, soft-paste and very much in the Mennecy style (Fig. 26). After his departure in 1769, Swedish porcelain changed to a hybrid body, and in 1777 a true hard-paste porcelain was produced. Though tastefully executed, these products lack originality, echoing the Copenhagen royal factory, through which the influence of Sèvres permeates in a dominant overtone.

Hunger, having failed to give any satisfaction to the King of Denmark, travelled on through Berlin and was finally engaged by the Empress of Russia, Elizabeth Petrova, in 1744, but after four years of unsuccessful experiments Hunger was dismissed from St Petersburg. With the accession of the Empress Catherine II in 1762 the manufacture of a hard-paste porcelain began in earnest, and an expert potter, Regensburg, was enticed from Vienna to direct operations. The style of the products was eclectic, and versions of German, Viennese and French porcelain can be found throughout the Catherine II period (1762–96).

MacCarthy, the Irishman, who had only a limited success in Copenhagen, started a factory at Weesp in Holland in 1757, which was firmly established by Count van Gronsveld-Diepenbroick in 1759. Hard-paste porcelain was made, but not without help from some of the Meissen workmen driven into exile by the Seven Years' War. The products are very white and of exceptionally good quality, based largely on the German in matters of form and decoration. In 1771 the factory was bought up by a pastor named Johannes de Mol, who had it transferred in its entirety to Oude Loosdrecht, where it flourished until his death in 1782. One of the most ambitious examples of enamelling at the factory is by N. Wicart (Plate 51). This treatment of porcelain as if it were a canvas for the painter is in accordance with the fashion set by the painters at Sèvres (Plate 42). The factory did not continue at this level after it

had been bought up and transferred in 1784 to Amstel, near Amsterdam.

Tournai, now in Belgium but in the eighteenth century part of the Austrian Netherlands, possessed the first and only soft-paste porcelain manufactory in Germanic territory. Founded under the patronage of the Empress Maria Theresa in 1751 and given financial help by the Governors of the Low Countries, the Tournai factory was nevertheless French in every other way. Run by Francois-Joseph Peterinck, a businessman from Lille, the factory relied for the secret of making porcelain on Robert Dubois, a potter from Chantilly and Vincennes.

From 1755, the porcelain developed a faintly creamy tone and a purity of texture that puts it among the best. The earlier products are imitations of Vincennes, Sèvres and Meissen patterns; thereafter a close connection with English porcelain can frequently be discerned. English workmen are known to have been engaged at Tournai in 1754 and 1759. The excellent 'exotic bird' decoration of the chief painter, Henri-Joseph Duvivier (1763–71), recalls his earlier work at Chelsea. Indeed, much of Tournai porcelain has the same restraint and neat quality that characterises Worcester and Derby porcelains. In the field of figures, there is an even closer resemblance; the modeller, Joseph Willems, worked in a leading capacity at both Chelsea (Plate 35) and Tournai. Nicolas Gauron, a modeller from Mennecy and Vincennes, worked at Tournai from 1758 and later at Chelsea. The figures attributed to the modeller Nicolas Lecreux, however, have a distinctive miniature delicacy and slender crispness that is unique in European porcelain and characteristic of much of the best Tournai figure subjects (Plate 50). Lecreux was born at Valenciennes in 1733 and achieved success as a sculptor as well as a modeller at Tournai. This factory acted in many ways as a link between the Continent and England in the field of porcelain-making.

Porcelain in England

Unlike most of the Continental factories, which were founded under the patronage of a sovereign ruler, however small the state, with all the attendant financial aids and privileges of monopoly, the English porcelain factories received no royal patronage, no special privileges or monopolistic concessions. The English factories are unique in being the creations of businessmen of relatively modest means and were clearly run on a strictly commercial basis with no consideration of national prestige or courtly rivalry.

All English porcelain until 1768 was an artificial soft-paste porcelain. The earliest date on any piece of English porcelain is '1745'; it appears on the so-called 'goat and bee' jugs, one of which, marked with the incised triangle, is inscribed 'Chelsea 1745' (now in the British Museum) (Fig. 27). No records survive to establish when or how the Chelsea porcelain factory was started, but prior to 1749 the 'Proprietor' and Chief Manager' was Charles Gouyn, a Belgian silversmith. By 1749 the manager was another Belgian, Nicholas Sprimont, a silversmith from Liège, who may have been a subsidiary partner at the commencement. The chief backer was probably Sir Everard Fawkener, secretary to William, Duke of Cumberland, whose patronage, no doubt, aided the factory. When Sir Everard Fawkener died in 1758, Sprimont became the owner, and only in 1769 did Sprimont sell the factory; it was then merged with the Derby factory of William Duesbury in 1770, but closed in 1784.

Not surprisingly, therefore, the early Chelsea productions, which are mainly tablewares in the white, are copied from silver shapes. By the late forties, a brilliant enamelled palette of very limited range had been achieved, as can be seen on the Baroque silver-shaped milk-jug (Plate 28). About 1749 there was evidently internal strife in the factory, and a break-away element set up a rival factory in Chelsea, which survived for a few years only, during which time it produced a distinctive group of figures, known to collectors as 'The Girl in the Swing Group'. The modeller of these figures produced refined elegance that is unnaturalistic, but nevertheless full of charm. Usually found in the white, there are a few pieces enamelled in a res-

trained and delicate way (Plate 28). Many of the famous 'Chelsea Toys' (scent-bottles, snuff-boxes, patch-boxes, etc.) were not made at Sprimont's Chelsea factory but at the subsidiary Chelsea factory in the early 1750s.

Whilst much of Sprimont's Chelsea tableware of the 1750s is strongly influenced by Vincennes-Sèvres, both in form and decoration, there developed at Chelsea a figure style which can only be described as a distinctive 'factory style', due to the leadership of the modeller, Joseph Willems, who had come from Tournai to Chelsea at least by 1755, if not earlier. In his 'Maypole Group' (Plate 35) the figures have a strong Flemish peasant strain in them, but because most of his Chelsea figures are closely copied from engravings, even seventeenth-century prints, his individual style is often overshadowed by the style of the artist whose work he is copying. Consequently Joseph Willems does not emerge as a great modeller in the way that Kaendler and Bustelli do. By 1760, the delicate Chelsea style disappeared in a riot of sumptuous coloured grounds with elaborately tooled gilt decoration and painted figure-scenes (Plate 44). In general this change was due to the overwhelming influence of Sèvres, either direct or through Tournai. The forms are usually elaborate Rococo, though occasionally there is an early and rare appearance of the disciplined neo-classical style.

In the seven years between 1745 and 1752 at least seven porcelain factories sprang up in England, but none approached the same degree of excellence found in the best of Chelsea. The most English of these factories, in which rather less Continental influence can be detected, is the China Works at Bow. Situated in the East End of London, just east of Bow Bridge, this factory, under Thomas Frye, was producing on a commercial scale by 1747, though experiments had been begun by him as early as 1744.

Thomas Frye was a canvas painter, born near Dublin in 1710, and is still ranked among the better British mezzotint-engravers of the eighteenth century. Why and how he became caught up in the excitement to discover the mystery of porcelain-making is not clear, but he was the first man to

Plate 48
Chinese dancers, modelled by Domenico Ferretti at Ludwigsburg about 1770. Ht. 30.5 cm. (12 in.). *British Museum, London.*

Plate 49
Table-centre of architectural form incorporating fifteen shell dishes; made at Zürich about 1775. Ht. 61.0 cm. (24 in.). *Victoria and Albert Museum, London.*

Pl. 48

Pl. 49

make a porcelain with a bone-ash, or phosphatic content, in 1747. By adding bone-ash, he produced a soft-paste porcelain of far greater durability, with a far lower percentage of kiln failures. Bow porcelain was, therefore, the first 'bone-china' ever produced; 'bone-china' was, and still is, the great English contribution to the world of porcelain-making – even Chelsea adapted its recipe to include bone-ash soon after Sprimont gained complete control in 1758.

Frye, at the commencement, secured the financial backing of a City businessman, Alderman George Arnold, a bachelor, who was a linen-draper near St Paul's. They evidently fell under the spell of the current wave of *chinoiserie* that was the vogue in London, for some Bow commemorative pieces made in 1750 and 1751 are inscribed: 'Made at New Canton', and an account written by one of the painters at the factory records that 'the Model of the Building was taken from that at Canton in China: the whole was heated by 2 Stoves, on the outside of the Building, and conveyed through Flews or Pipes, and warmed the whole, sometimes to an intense heat, unbearable in Winter . . .'

The striking feature of the early products of this factory, like those of Chelsea (Plate 32), is that the decoration, whether enamelled or in underglaze blue, is largely Oriental in origin. In the realm of figures, the factory did copy a number of Meissen models as early as 1750, but the majority were original creations copied from engravings, both contemporary and seventeenth-century prints, as was the practice of Willems at Chelsea. Like Chelsea, however, Bow was apparently more closely in touch with contemporary life in London, for its figures of victorious generals, or London's actors and actresses in roles that were current 'hits', evince a lively awareness of popular feeling. However, figure groups based on prints after Watteau and Boucher were, undoubtedly, among the most popular (Fig. 28), and although the early enamelling at Bow is not subtle it has a naiveté and a rich vibrant tone that is unique (Plate 26).

After Thomas Frye's retirement in 1759, the factory's products, which had achieved a remarkably high standard and a most individual character, began to lose their quality of liveliness, and slowly a monotonous, indeterminate mediocrity crept into the output of the late 1760s. The factory was sold to William Duesbury of Derby in 1776, six years after

he had bought up the Chelsea factory, but in the case of Bow all production ceased with the take-over. So ended a remarkable factory that had enjoyed a large export trade to North American colonies and had employed about 300 craftsmen at its zenith in 1760 – almost as many as were employed in the royal factory at Sèvres.

Tradition says that by working at Bow as a potter, Robert Browne of Lowestoft learnt the secret of making bone-ash porcelain and so was able to return to his Suffolk home-town in 1757 and establish the local porcelain factory, which did not close until 1802. The manufactory was never large, having at most about seventy employees, but its long life has left behind an abundance of examples of its products, none of which bears a factory mark – only copies of the marks of other factories! Certainly Lowestoft china was from the beginning almost identical with Bow, and because much of it is decorated in underglaze blue with Oriental motifs, like Bow china, the difficulties of distinguishing it from Bow are among the delightful pangs that torture the enthusiastic collector. The coloured wares are easily recognised, as the distinctive palette of reddish brown, bright turquoise, blue and green

Fig. 29
Engraving, *La Muse Erato*, by J. Daullé after Boucher, 1756.

Fig. 30
'The Muse Erato'; porcelain figure made at Derby about 1760 and copied from the engraving after Boucher's painting (see Fig. 29). This figure and the Muse Clio (Plate 45) form a pair. Ht. 22 cm. (8¾ in.). *British Museum, London.*

Plate 50
Goat, made at William Cookworthy's factory in Plymouth about 1768. Like so much of the earliest Cookworthy porcelain, the goat is marred by smoke-staining caused during firing; it is, however, the earliest hard-paste or true porcelain to be made in England. Ht. 9.5 cm. (3¾ in.). Boy leading a horse, made at Tournai (Belgium) about 1760. Probably modelled by Nicolas Lecreux. Ht. 12.1 cm. (4¾ in.). *Both in the British Museum, London.*

Plate 51
Panel, from the centre of a large dish, made at Oude Loosdrecht, (near Amsterdam) about 1770–80 and painted by N. Wicart with the Siege of Graave by Prince Maurits in 1602 from the engraving after S. Fokke. Mark: M:OL (in blue and incised). Width (inside frame) 32.5 cm. (12¾ in.). *British Museum, London.*

is used in an unusual mannerism of style that is rather stereotyped and limited in range. The factory hardly attempted to produce figures, but a few very small-scale works, toys such as cats and dogs and swans, were made in the late 1770s (Plate 29).

Although 'the Potteries' in Staffordshire were a flourishing centre of ceramic production in the first half of the eighteenth century, no attempt was made by the local manufacturers to make porcelain until the mid-forties. The first successful commercial venture began in 1749 when William Jenkinson, a gentleman from London with mining interests, set up a factory in the grounds of Longton Hall, a few miles from Stoke. With the help of a young local potter, William Littler and his wife, Jane, a decorator, Jenkinson succeeded in producing porcelain figures and tablewares as early as 1750. By 1753, Jenkinson's interest in porcelain ended, but new partners joined the expanding concern, and for ten years the factory continued with a remarkable variety and highly individual range of designs. Steadily improving, the factory really reached a high degree of accomplishment by the time Littler was forced by his partner, Robert Charlesworth, to close in 1760. The famous equestrian figure of the Duke of Brunswick in the British Museum is an elegant and graceful achievement for so small a factory, but although many of its tablewares are decorated in a simplicity that accords with present-day taste, the general tendency was towards excess (Plate 36) – rather like an unattended country garden!

William Duesbury, who was born in Staffordshire in 1725 and died one of the major manufacturers of English porcelain, began as an enameller of white porcelain in the late forties. His workshop was in London and his workbooks for 1751–53, which have fortunately survived, prove that porcelain from the Chelsea, Bow, Derby and Staffordshire (Longton Hall) factories was sent there for decorating, especially the figures. The entries in his workbooks are the only written proof of the existence of Derby porcelain before 1756. In that year the Derby factory was established under three partners, John Heath, a businessman of Derby, Andrew Planché, a porcelain-maker who had come from London to Derby in about 1750, and William Duesbury, who had from 1754 been an enameller at the Longton Hall factory. With his father's capital he was able in 1756 to enter the porcelain manufacturing field as a partner. Later, Duesbury assumed complete control and was obviously so successful as a businessman that he could buy out his rivals, Chelsea (1770) and Bow (1776), and establish the Derby China Works on so sound a basis that despite many setbacks it survived until 1848 as one of the largest china works in England.

The Derby factory advertised the sale of its products in 1757 as 'the largest variety of the Derby or second Dresden factory' and in 1758 announced the sale of 'great variety of Figures, the nearest to Dresden'. Duesbury's great aim was to rival the imported porcelain from Meissen, but the quality seldom approached Chelsea, let alone Meissen. The chalky quality in the paste, together with the bluish tinge in the glaze, are frequent detractions, and although the earlier small figures have a stiff doll-like charm, the trend to large-scale figures by 1760 emphasised the gauche, clumsy modelling. The more faithfully, or rather slavishly, the Meissen models were copied, the more successful the results. As early as 1760, modellers at Derby occasionally attempted original productions, by copying French engravings after artists like Watteau and Boucher. One of these rare examples (Plate 45) is a pair of figures representing the Clio and Erato, as painted by Boucher (Figs. 29 and 30).

From about 1770, the influence of Sèvres was the dominant factor and Derby was the one English factory that produced biscuit figures in vast quantities in the manner of the Sèvres. These figures, produced from about 1773 onwards, are in the neo-classical taste, but some of the modellers were gifted, outstanding among whom was John James Spangler, the son of the director of the Zürich porcelain factory. During the first half of the nineteenth century, a number of good painters, like William Corden, worked at Derby at a time when there was a vogue in England for porcelain plaques painted with portraits, landscapes or still-life subjects in the manner of contemporary oil-paintings.

William Billingsley, one of the most gifted of the decorators at Derby from 1775 to 1796, left to establish a porcelain factory at Pinxton in Derbyshire. After three years he left there and eventually started a factory at Nantgarw, near Cardiff in 1813. The following year it was transferred to Swansea, but in 1817 Billingsley was back in Nantgarw. In 1820, Billingsley took his secret recipe to the factory at Coalport on the River Severn. From his recipe a glossy soft-paste of very beautiful quality was made at all four factories but was so exceedingly unstable in the kiln that it was liable to melt out of shape and in consequence was hopelessly expensive to produce.

After an unsuccessful attempt to establish a porcelain factory at Limehouse in the East End of London during the mid-forties, the proprietor (as yet unidentified) tried again in Bristol in about 1748–50 with Benjamin Lund, a local manufacturer. For two years Lund's Bristol porcelain factory produced a soft-paste china that is often faulty, but when enamelled is of the greatest delicacy and charm (Plate 29). Then in 1752 Lund's factory was merged with the new China Works at Worcester, established at Warmstry House only the year before. The merger involved the moving of all the moulds and many of the personnel from Bristol to Worcester, with the result that there can be no clear-cut distinction between Lund's Bristol porcelain and early Worcester products. Both factories were almost exclusively concerned with the making of table-wares and both used in their porcelain recipes a new ingredient, Cornish soapstone (steatite), which greatly reduced the risk of breakage that might be caused by sudden changes in temperature.

The greyish appearance of the porcelain in the first decade of its long life offers an attractive background for the enamelling of European scenes and decorative motifs by the factory's several gifted painters, such as James Rogers (Plate 40). The copying of Chinese patterns, and to a lesser extent of Japanese patterns, was the aim at first, but quickly the endless variations on these themes were commenced, often with great taste and originality, and always with a high standard of execution. The Worcester factory is the only one from amongst the seven English porcelain works that began in the middle of the eighteenth century which still functions today. Its productions have survived in great quantity, but although the variety of patterns and decoration on the tablewares seems endless, the absence of any large-scale attempt at figures is disappointing for the collector.

Soapstone porcelain, which frequently seems almost as hard as true hard-paste porcelain, was only made at two other centres in England, at Liverpool and at Caughley (Shropshire), both off-shoots of the Worcester factory.

Liverpool had many small potteries, at least seven of which produced porcelain, though attempts to identify them have only partially succeeded. The most important, however, was undoubtedly the factory started in 1754 by Richard Chaffers with the aid of the potter Robert Podmore, who had moved from Lund's Bristol factory to Worcester in 1751. Often the enamelling is distinctive, for the freedom of the brushwork recalls the painting on local 'delft-ware' (Plate 41). Much of the porcelain was, however, decorated with that singularly English mode of ornament, the transfer-print (Plate 41). The design, minutely engraved in reverse on a copper plate, is taken off in enamel pigment on paper and transferred to the surface of the porcelain, and then fired. This technique was first evolved in England soon after 1750 on enamels, for example at Battersea (London) in 1753, and then spread to porcelain – Bow (1754), Worcester (1756) and Liverpool (1756). John Sadler and Guy Green's printing works in

Liverpool were the biggest in this field; and in the Potteries, Wedgwood started the fashion for transfer-printing on earthenware by sending his cream-ware to Liverpool for this decoration. Though Continental factories followed suit, the taste for it never 'caught on', whereas in England it was practised without a break throughout the nineteenth century to the present day.

The first English hard-paste, or true, porcelain was made in Devon in 1768, sixty years after von Tschirnhaus had met with success at Dresden. But it was made with English supplies of kaolin and petuntse, found in Cornwall by William Cook-worthy of Plymouth. His Plymouth factory was transferred to Bristol after two years and, being a man of almost seventy, he sold it to Richard Champion in 1773, who renamed it the Bristol China Manufactory. Finanacial difficulties, largely due to the opposition organised by Josiah Wedgwood, forced Champion to sell out in 1781 to a group of Staffordshire potters, who transferred the works to New Hall, near Stoke-on-Trent. There is little to distinguish the products of Plymouth from the early porcelain of Bristol, and both suffer from a tendency to smoke-staining and other kiln defects (Plate 50). The glaze is glitteringly cold and brittle, and the body itself is not unlike a very hard glass. Many of the Plymouth figures are made from moulds identical to those used at Longton Hall, but occasionally figures of good design and simplicity were created. Although many splendid large services were made at Bristol for Champion's friends, like Edmund Burke, the large-scale sets of figures, the 'Continents', the 'Seasons', etc. (Plates 53, 54), were its most ambitious achievements. Without any special patronage or protective barriers, this hard-paste porcelain factory could not hope – any more than its parallels on the Continent – to be a commercial success, and so English true porcelain had a very short life of only twelve years.

Towards the end of the eighteenth century, Josiah Spode, of Stoke-on-Trent, produced a hybrid bone-porcelain, combining the essential ingredients of hard-paste with bone-ash. So manageable was this new composition, that it was soon generally adopted and Staffordshire bone-porcelain ('bone-china') has to this day supplied a world-wide market.

Pl. 53

Pl. 54

Plate 52
Pair of vases, made at Sèvres in 1781 with the rare so-called (jewelling), coloured enamel fused over gold or silver foil. Mark: interlaced Ls enclosing date letters DD (for 1781). The subject after Eisen (on the left-hand vase) is from Montesquieu's 'Temple de Cnide'; the Apollo and Leucothea subject (on the right-hand vase) is after Monnet. Ht. 31.8 cm. (12½ in.). *British Museum, London.*

Plates 53, 54
Pair of figures, Milkmaid and Goatherd, made in Bristol about 1775 of hard-paste porcelain, perhaps modelled by Pierre Stephan. Goatherd: Ht. 27.6 cm. (10⅞ in.). Milkmaid: Ht. 26.0 cm. (10¼ in.). *Fenton House, Hampstead, London.*

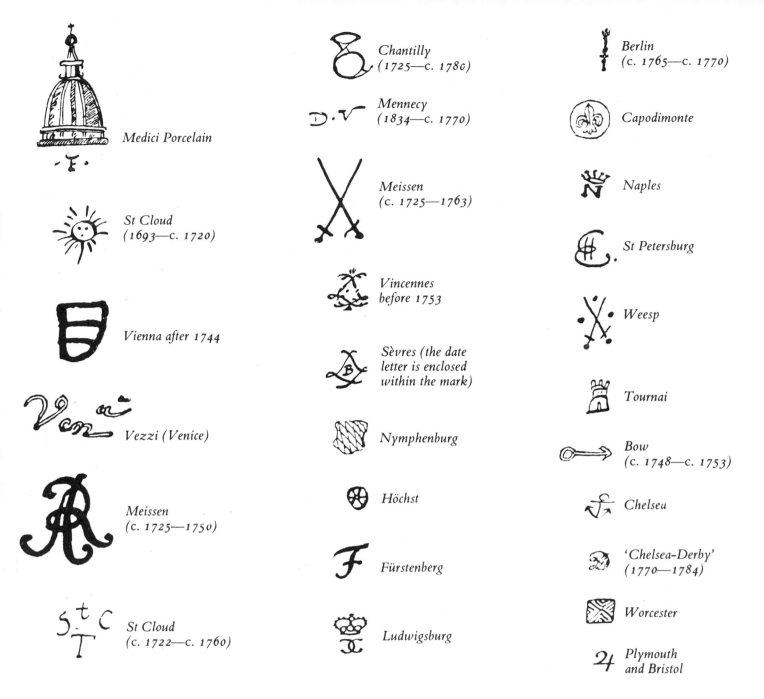

Medici Porcelain

St Cloud
(1693—c. 1720)

Vienna after 1744

Vezzi (Venice)

Meissen
(c. 1725—1750)

St Cloud
(c. 1722—c. 1760)

Chantilly
(1725—c. 1780)

Mennecy
(1834—c. 1770)

Meissen
(c. 1725—1763)

Vincennes
before 1753

Sèvres (the date
letter is enclosed
within the mark)

Nymphenburg

Höchst

Fürstenberg

Ludwigsburg

Berlin
(c. 1765—c. 1770)

Capodimonte

Naples

St Petersburg

Weesp

Tournai

Bow
(c. 1748—c. 1753)

Chelsea

'Chelsea-Derby'
(1770—1784)

Worcester

Plymouth
and Bristol

Porcelain Marks

Factory Marks–Note of Warning

Factory marks are by themselves of very limited use to the collector or student as a means of identifying the porcelain–they are too untrustworthy.

A very few examples of the more reliable marks are reproduced here, but until the nineteenth century the practice of marking the products of each factory was by no means universal nor were many of the factories that had a mark consistent in their use of it. Many products would leave a factory unmarked, especially in the early decades of a factory's life. Other porcelain factories used a variety of marks, even during the same period. Many of the lesser factories used a slight variation of a major factory's mark, such as Weesp's version of Meissen's crossed swords mark, in the hope that their products

might pass for the more expensive wares of the superior factory.

Forgeries of marks are not unknown on porcelain made within the last hundred years in imitation of the earlier porcelain prized by collectors. In other cases, mediocre eighteenth-century porcelain is richly redecorated in the nineteenth century and a bogus mark added. Marks put on by the potter or the decorator for use within the factory are often misleading or confusing for the newcomer–indeed, marks are only an aid when allied to a full knowledge of the characteristics which distinguish the porcelain of one factory from that of another.

Bibliography

Charles, Rollo. *Continental Porcelain of the Eighteenth Century*, London, 1964.

Charleston, R. J. (editor). *English Porcelain, 1745–1850*, London, 1965.

Charleston, R. J. (editor). *World Ceramics*, London, 1968.

Dingwall, Kenneth. *The Derivation of some Kakiemon Designs on Porcelain*, London, 1926.

Ducret, Siegfried. *German Porcelain and Faience*, New York, 1962.

Hillier, Bevis. *Pottery and Porcelain, 1700–1914*, London, 1968.

Honey, W. B. *Dresden China*, London, 1954.

Honey, W. B. *French Porcelain of the Eighteenth Century*, London, 1950.

Honey, W. B. *European Ceramic Art*, Vol. I, London (2nd edition), 1963.

Honour, Hugh. *Chinoiserie: The Vision of Cathay*, New York, 1962.

Jenyns, Soame. *Japanese Porcelain*, London, 1965.

Jenyns, Soame. *Ming Pottery and Porcelain*, London, 1953.

Lane, Arthur. *English Porcelain Figures of the Eighteenth Century*, London, 1961.

Lane, Arthur. *Italian Porcelain*, London, 1954.

Reitlinger, Gerald. *The Economics of Taste*, 3 vols. London, 1961–70.

Schmidt, Robert. *Porcelain as an Art and a Mirror of Fashion*, London, 1932.

Volker, T. *The Japanese Porcelain Trade of the Dutch East India Company after 1683*, Leiden, 1959.

Acknowledgements

Plate 35 is reproduced by permission of the Syndics of the Fitzwilliam Museum, Cambridge, figure 24 by permission of Patrimonio Nacional, Madrid and plates 23 and 37 and figure 18 by permission of the Trustees of the Wallace Collection, London.

Sources of Photographs

Colour
Fitzwilliam Museum, Cambridge 35; Hamlyn Picture Library 2, 3, 4, 5, 6, 7, 8, 9, 10, 11, 12, 13, 14, 15, 17, 19, 20, 21, 22, 23, 26, 27, 28, 29, 30, 31, 32, 33, 34, 36, 37, 39, 40, 41, 42, 43, 44, 45, 46, 47, 48, 49, 50, 51, 52, 53, 54, 55, jacket; Hessisches Landesmuseum, Kassel 1; Cecil Higgins Museum, Bedford 25, 38; Musée des Arts Décoratifs, Paris 16, 18, 24.

Black and white
Alinari, Florence 23; British Museum, London 29; Fondazione Giorgio Cini, Venice 1; Deutsche Fotothek Dresden 15; Dr S. Ducret, Zurich 7, 12; Photographie Giraudon, Paris 2; Hamlyn Group Picture Library 16; Hamlyn Group–Hawkley Studio Associates 5, 8, 9, 17, 19, 20, 21, 22, 25, 26, 27, 28, 30; Kunstbibliothek, Berlin 10; MAS, Barcelona 24; Musée National de Céramique, Sèvres 6; National Museum of Ireland, Dublin 3; Sotheby and Co., London 11, 13, 14; Victoria and Albert Museum, London 4; Wallace Collection, London 18.

Plate 55
Temple of Bacchus, hard–paste porcelain, made in Berlin towards the end of eighteenth century. Mark: a sceptre in underglaze blue. Ht. 58.5 cm. (23 in.). *Victoria and Albert Museum, London.*

Index

Numbers in **bold** refer to black and white illustrations and those in *italics* to colour illustrations